The
Life and Way
for the
Practice
of the
Church
Life

Witness Lee

Living Stream Ministry
Anaheim, California

First Edition, 4,200 copies. July 1994.

ISBN 0-87083-785-0

Published by

Living Stream Ministry
1853 W. Ball Road, Anaheim, CA 92804 U.S.A.
P. O. Box 2121, Anaheim, CA 92814 U.S.A.

Printed in the United States of America

CONTENTS

PREFACE

This book is composed of messages given by Brother Witness Lee in Los Angeles, California in the winter of 1963.

he univ. needs God! God is made available in Christ. + Christ is made real in The church. Christ is so rich to us because of the church.

(Life) One New Man
(Husband) WIFE
(Dweller) house, Tab, Temple — rest!
(Ruler) city
(Commander) army
(Head) Body
(Reality) Fullness
(Content) Great Corporate Vessel
(Lamp) Lampstand

Because the Lord is so much, He wants The church To be all that He is, not in the Godhead but in expressing Him.
Key to hapiness is to Take care of the church.

CHAPTER ONE

THE POSITION OF THE CHURCH IN GOD'S ECONOMY

Scripture Reading: Matt. 16:15-19; Eph. 5:32

The burden of the fellowship in this book is twofold. On the one hand, we will cover the building up of the Body of Christ, and on the other hand, we will take care of the urgent need today among the Lord's children. Hence, the subject of this book is the life and way for the church practice.

I look to the Lord that He will help us see the practice of the church. First, we have to realize that to have any kind of practice, there is the need of a certain kind of life. If you have the life, you have the practice. If you do not have the life, it is impossible for you to have any practice. After you have the life, you need the way, the method, for the practice. The life is the power, the strength, whereas the way is the method. In order to have any kind of practice, we need the life as well as the way. With the Lord's help, we will cover the life for the practice of the church and the way to practice it.

Now let us read Matthew 16:15-19: "He [Jesus] said to them, But you, who do you say that I am? And Simon Peter answered and said, You are the Christ, the Son of the living God. And Jesus answered and said to him, Blessed are you, Simon Barjona, because flesh and blood has not revealed this to you, but My Father who is in the heavens. And I also say to you that you are Peter, and upon this rock I will build My church, and the gates of Hades shall not prevail against it. I will give to you the keys of the kingdom of the heavens, and whatever you bind on the earth shall have been bound in the heavens, and whatever you loose on the earth shall have been loosed in the heavens." In verse 18, *Peter* means a little rock, a stone; *this rock* refers to Christ with the living and real knowledge of Him. Christ will build His church upon Himself as the Son of God and upon the living and real knowledge of Him. In this portion of the Word, we have Christ, the church, Hades, and the kingdom of the heavens.

Let us also read Ephesians 5:32: "This mystery is great, but I speak with regard to Christ and the church." The great mystery is concerning Christ and the church.

THE HEAD AND THE BODY

Before we go on to see something concerning the practice of the church, I have the burden to lay a foundation by pointing out the position of the church in God's economy. If we human beings have our economy, then surely God has His economy. In the divine economy, the church has a tremendous position.

Many times I was told that Christ is the center of the holy Scriptures. Although I admit that this is true, I would say that the center of the Scriptures is not just Christ Himself. Christ as the center of the Bible is the Head. Physically speaking, we all know that with the head there is the body. You cannot have just the head and forget about the body. The Bible shows us a great man, a universal man (Col. 3:10-11). This universally great man is Christ with His church. Christ Himself is the Head of this man, and His church is the Body of this man. Therefore, we have to realize that the center of the Scriptures is not just Christ but Christ with His Body, the church.

You cannot remove the church from the Scriptures. If you have Christ as the Head, surely you have the church as His Body. It is impossible for me to go somewhere with just my head and leave my body in my house. Yet some people would argue by saying, "Let us talk only about Christ. Don't talk about the church." But it is not right to say this. If you are going to speak about Christ, surely you have to say something about the church.

In Matthew 16 the Lord first spoke about Himself by asking His disciples who He is. Peter said, "You are the Christ, the Son of the living God" (v. 16). After Peter received this revelation, this knowledge, immediately the Lord told him that He would build His church upon this rock—Christ Himself with the living knowledge of Him. The church will be built upon the living Christ with the living knowledge of Him. Here we see the principle. If you talk about Christ, then you have to know the church. If you have the Head, you must have the Body.

THE LINE OF CHRIST WITH THE CHURCH IN THE SCRIPTURES

Now I want to help us see that throughout the Scriptures, there is the line of Christ with the church. There is the line of the church always going together with Christ. There is the church as the counterpart of Christ.

In the Old Testament

In the very first chapter of the Bible, there is a man created by God. The created man, Adam, was not only an individual man but also an inclusive man, a corporate man (1 Cor. 15:22). Adam as the inclusive man was created in the image of God (Gen. 1:26). In Colossians 1:15 we are told that Christ is the image of the invisible God. Hence, for man to be created according to the image of God simply means that man was created according to Christ. Why did God create a man? What was His purpose? God's purpose was that man would be the material for the formation and building up of the Body of Christ.

In the second chapter of the Scriptures there is a wife. After He created Adam, God said, "It is not good that the man should be alone" (Gen. 2:18). In other words, it was not good for man to be single. There was the need for man to have a wife, so God created Eve. Eve is a type of the church (Eph. 5:31-32), and Adam is a type of Christ (Rom. 5:14b). Eve came out of Adam and went back to Adam to be one with Adam as one body. In the New Testament we are told that the church is the counterpart of Christ, the bride of Christ (Eph. 5:24-25; John 3:29).

Later in the Scriptures there is the house of God. In Genesis 28, Jacob came to a certain place where he had a dream and saw a vision, and he called the name of that place Bethel, which means the house of God (vv. 11-19). The house of God is the church (1 Tim. 3:15).

When we go on further, we see a tabernacle (Exo. 25:8-9; 40:2). That tabernacle was not merely a tabernacle made of material things; it signified all the children of Israel as a dwelling place of God.

After the tabernacle, there was the temple. There are a lot of types in the Old Testament, and the temple is the last and the fullest of them all.

In the Old Testament, there is also the city. At the end of Ezekiel, there is a city with twelve gates (48:30-35). It has three gates on each side, which is exactly the same as the New Jerusalem (Rev. 21:16, 12-13).

Besides the man, the bride, the house, the tabernacle, the temple, and the city in the Old Testament, the children of Israel were formed together as an army to fight for the kingdom of God (Num. 1:1-3).

If we take away these few items—the man, the wife, the house, the tabernacle, the temple, the city, and the army—from the Old Testament, the Old Testament becomes empty. The whole Old Testament is a record of these few items.

In the New Testament

Now we come to the New Testament. The first person we see is Christ Himself, the God-man, the Son of God incarnated as a man. But when we get into the knowledge of Him, He would let us know that there is a need for us to know the church. If you are one of those who, like Peter, know Christ as the Son of the living God, you have to realize the building up of the church.

After the Gospels, there is the building up of the church. From the second chapter of Acts to the last chapter of the New Testament, one thing is dealt with, that is, the church. The church is a man, a new man (Eph. 2:15). The church is the bride, the wife, of Christ (5:24-25). The church is the house of God (1 Tim. 3:15), the tabernacle of God (Rev. 21:3), the temple of God (Eph. 2:21-22; 1 Cor. 3:16-17), the city of God (Rev. 21:2), and the army of God (Eph. 6:11-12).

Throughout all the generations, the church has been and still is fighting for God's kingdom.

Besides these seven items—the man, the wife, the house, the tabernacle, the temple, the city, and the army—there is the Body. This term is not found in the Old Testament; it is a new term in the New Testament. Ephesians 1:22 and 23 tell us that the church is the Body of Christ. We Christians are familiar with many of the biblical terms, but we probably do not know the right meaning of these terms. We may talk about the church being the Body of Christ, but I am afraid very few can tell us accurately what it means.

Actually, the Body of Christ is simply Christ Himself (1 Cor. 12:12). A person's body is the person himself. You cannot consider the person as one entity, and his body as another entity. The body is the very person; it is the main part of the person. Hence, the church as the Body of Christ is a part of Christ, even Christ Himself.

Ephesians 1:23 also tells us that the church as the Body of Christ is the fullness of Christ. The church is a great, universal, corporate vessel, a great container, to contain the very Triune God—the Father, the Son, and the Spirit. The Triune God is the content of the church as the divine container, the divine corporate vessel. Eventually, in Revelation, the church is a lampstand (1:11-12, 20). If you took away these eleven items—the man, the wife, the house, the tabernacle, the temple, the city, the army, the Body, the fullness, the vessel, and the lampstand—from the Bible, it would become an empty book.

Christ is the image and life of the church. In Genesis 1 is the image of God (v. 26), and in chapter two is the tree of life (v. 9). We need the image and the life. The image is Christ Himself. The church is in the form, the image, of Christ Himself, and the life of the church is Christ Himself. Also, the church as a wife needs Christ as the Husband, the Bridegroom.

With a house, there is the need of a dweller. If you have a house and nobody dwells in it, it is an empty house. The church is the house, and Christ, the embodiment of the Triune God, is the Inhabitant, the Dweller. With the tabernacle and the temple, it is the same. With a city, there is the need of government, of ruling. The city needs a ruler. Who is the Ruler of the church as the city of God? This Ruler is Christ, the King of kings (Rev. 1:5; 17:14). Now we come to the need of the army. The army needs a commander, a general. Christ is the Commander of the church as the army of God.

The church as the Body of Christ needs Christ as the Head. With the fullness, there is the need of the reality. Christ is the reality of the church as His fullness. Then with the vessel, the container, there is the need of the content. Christ is the content of the church as the vessel, the container. Finally, with a lampstand, there is the need of a lamp. In Revelation we are told that God as the light is in Christ as the lamp, and the church is the lampstand, the lamp bearer, the lamp holder (21:23; 22:5). The church as the lampstand holds and bears Christ as the lamp shining with God as the light.

GOD'S DESIRE FOR THE CHURCH, THE BODY OF CHRIST

If we bring all these things to the Lord and spend some time to consider them, we will be clear about the position of the church in God's economy. We will see that what God is looking for and what He is working for is the church, the Body of Christ. But throughout all the generations the enemy has been doing his best to spoil, frustrate, damage, and even destroy this church. Look at the situation of Christianity today. There are thousands and even millions of Christians, but it is not easy to point out a group of believers practicing the church life in a proper way.

Suppose you come to Los Angeles or go to New York. We all know that in these big cities there are millions of Christians. But where can you find the proper church? Throughout all the generations this has been a real problem, and it is still a problem today. It is a problem because the church is what God is looking for and working for, and it is also what the enemy hates, spoils, damages, and frustrates. The enemy tries to cover and even to bury the matter of the church. But we believe that in these last days the Lord is going to recover the church life.

The church is the bride to the Bridegroom, and without the bride, there is no way and no purpose for the Bridegroom to come back. Christ will be able to come back by the bride's being prepared. As long as the bride is not ready, the Bridegroom cannot come back for her. In the book of Revelation, we are told that when the bride is ready, prepared, the Bridegroom will come back (19:7). This is why we have the assurance that in these last days the Lord is going to recover the church life to prepare His bride.

CHRIST AS LIFE FOR THE CHURCH

What is the life for us to practice the church, and what is the proper way for us to practice the church life? These are the problems. The burden today is to meet the urgent need by helping us to see the life and the way for the church practice. No doubt, we all would say that the life for us to practice the church is Christ Himself. Many of us have the realization that we need Christ as our life, but very few realize that Christ as our life is for us to practice the church life.

There have been many teachings about life—the victorious life, the sanctified life, the exchanged life, the crucified life, the spiritual life, the divine life, the eternal life, and the life of Christ, the life of God. But it is hard to find a book telling us that this overcoming life, this spiritual life, the life of Christ, is for the church. This life is not just for victory or for sanctification. This life is not just for being spiritual, divine, and holy. This life is for a definite purpose, that is, for the building up of the church as the Body of Christ. Simply speaking, this life is for the church.

For what purpose do you want to be victorious or sanctified? For what purpose do you want to be divine, spiritual, or holy? Look at a building. Every piece of material has been dealt with and cut into a certain size and shape for the purpose of fitting the building. I have seen a number of truly spiritual people, and I did get some spiritual help from them. But one day the Lord asked me, "There are many spiritual persons as beautiful stones, beautiful materials, but where is the building?" You may be spiritually beautiful, but are you just a beautiful stone or have you been built together with others in the house? This is a problem.

In a certain place, I met a very spiritual person. But one day the Lord opened my eyes and asked me, "Do I need some individually spiritual persons, some beautiful individual pieces of stone, or do I need a house?" On that day, my eyes were opened and I bowed before the Lord, saying, "Lord, I want to be a stone that is built up with others. I realize You need a house. You do not need a lot of beautiful stones which are good for exhibition." What the Lord needs today is not many beautiful stones but a built-up house. While Jacob was wandering in the wilderness, in his dream he saw Bethel (Gen. 28:19). At that time Jacob was a homeless person, and God was a homeless God. What the Lord needs in this universe is a home, a house, a building, a church, a Body.

Suppose a person's two eyes are removed from his body. They are two individually beautiful eyes, but what is their use outside the body? In a sense, these two eyes are quite beautiful, yet in another sense, they are very peculiar. Honestly speaking, I have met a lot of Christians who are beautiful but who are also peculiar. They are spiritual yet individualistic. Maybe you have been a Christian for many years, but as a piece of material for God's building, with whom have you been built up and with whom are you really related? I am afraid you are either individually spiritual or spiritually individualistic.

I want to say again that the life of Christ is not just for victory, for sanctification, for being spiritual, or for being heavenly, but for His Body. The Lord can be fully realized as life to us only when we realize that we are members of the Body. When we realize that we are members of the Body and live as such members, we will know the fullness of Christ's being life to us.

OVERCOMING IN THE BODY

Let me give you a suggestion. Suppose you have a besetting sin which you cannot overcome. You have been trying and trying to overcome, yet you fail again and again. I suggest that you bring your failure, your problem, to the

Body. You will see right away that the victory is yours. Sometimes you may say that it is hard for you to be clear about the Lord's guidance. But if you would bring the matter to the Body and fellowship with the Body, you would be clear about the Lord's guidance.

Do you desire to have a sanctified life? Just bring yourself to the Body, and you will see that you have been sanctified already. It is easy for you to realize the fullness of Christ's being life to you if you put yourself in the Body. The isolated members are the poorest members. If you simply abide in the Body, all the fullness of the Body will be yours to enjoy.

Sometimes people have asked me, "Brother Lee, how do you study the Bible? How many hours and days have you spent in the Word so that you are able to receive this kind of light?" Many times I wish to answer, "I spend just a little time. I read the Word in the Body." One time I traveled to a certain place and ministered to the saints there. After a meeting, someone asked the brothers from which seminary I had graduated. I wish to let you know that I study in the "seminary" of the Body, and I have not graduated yet. I am still in the "university of the Body of Christ." This is my only university, and this is my only seminary. Day by day I learn something not only from the Bible and through the Bible but also from all the saints.

Another time, after I finished ministering to the saints in a certain locality, a brother came up to me, saying, "Brother Lee, we thank you for your ministry." I replied, "Brother, I thank you for your being here." This is because in the Body we learn more and more about the Lord. Just bring yourselves to the Body, and you will see where you are and how wonderful, how rich, and how full the blessing and the experience of Christ can be.

In these days, let us seek the Lord by praying in this way, "Lord, now I realize that Your central thought is the church for Christ. Teach me the proper way to practice the church life." I hope that you would pray much for this matter.

THE WHEEL OF GOD'S MOVE

In conclusion, I would like to point out that in Ezekiel

chapter one there are the wheels (vv. 15-21). These wheels represent the activity, the move, of the Lord. Today the wheels are the churches with Christ as their hub. Christ is the hub and the churches are the rim. Without Christ, there is no center. But without the church, there is no circumference. Without Christ, there is no hub; without the church, there is no rim. A wheel needs both the hub and the rim.

In this universe, with the wheel of God's move, God's activity, there is the need of the church as the rim to match Christ as the hub. When we have Christ as the center and the church as the rim, we will have the wheel of God moving all the time. One may have the strongest and the most beautiful hub, but if there is no rim, there is no wheel. Let us pray for God's move today. God needs to move on. With the divine move, there is the need of a hub, which is Christ Himself, and there is also the need of a rim, which is the church. If you have both the hub and the rim, then you have a wheel rolling on for God's move on the earth. May the Lord be merciful to us that we may see these things in a complete way. Christ is the hub, and the church is the rim.

12-25-94C

CHAPTER TWO

THE LIFE AND TRANSFORMATION
OF THE CHURCH

THE POSITION OF THE CHURCH

Matthew 13:45-46 says, "Again, the kingdom of the heavens is like a merchant seeking fine pearls; and finding one pearl of great value, he went and sold all that he had and bought it."

In Matthew 13 the Lord spoke seven parables. The parable concerning the pearl of great value is the sixth. These seven parables give us a full picture of this age until the Lord comes back. In this picture we can see where the church should stand. By these parables we can see the position of the church.

In order to help us understand the parable of the pearl of great value, we have to read Ephesians 5. Let us begin with verse 25: "Husbands, love your wives even as Christ also loved the church and gave Himself up for her." That merchant found a pearl and went and sold all that he had. This merchant signifies Christ who loved the church and gave Himself up for her. Verse 26 goes on to say, "That He might sanctify her, cleansing her by the washing of the water in the word." The washing of the water in the word is the washing of life, the divine life, the Spirit of life, the life-giving Spirit.

Then verses 27 through 32 say, "That He might present the church to Himself glorious, not having spot or wrinkle or any such things, but that she would be holy and without blemish....because we are members of His Body. For this cause a man shall leave his father and mother and shall be joined to his wife, and the two shall be one flesh. This mystery is great, but I speak with regard to Christ and the church."

This portion of the Word helps us to see the pearl of great value for which the Lord gave all that He had. This pearl of great value refers to the church. In the eyes of the Lord, the church is a pearl of great value.

Now we want to remind you of the eleven items which we saw in the previous chapter. First, in the Old Testament there are seven items: the man, the wife, the house, the tabernacle, the temple, the city, and the army. Then in the New Testament there are four items: the Body, the fullness, the vessel, and the lampstand. Eventually, the New Jerusalem is the twelfth item. The entire Scripture is a record of these twelve items. Actually, these eleven items added together equal the twelfth item, the last item, the New Jerusalem. The New Jerusalem is the ultimate consummation of the eleven items; it is the all-inclusive item.

Of course, the whole Scripture speaks about Christ as the embodiment of the Triune God (Col. 2:9). There is no doubt about this. This divine, heavenly book gives us a full revelation of the Triune God. It tells us that the Father is the source, the Son is the embodiment and the expression of the Father, and the Spirit is the transmission of the Son, the fellowship of the Father in the Son. It reveals to us the Triune God as life and everything to us. We will need our whole life, even all of eternity, to know and experience the Triune God, to experience God in Christ as the Spirit as life and everything to us.

However, we have to realize that for us to experience the Triune God in a full way, we need the church. This is just like saying a life needs a body, a husband needs a wife, a dweller needs a house, a commander needs an army, a ruler needs a city, the head needs a body, the reality needs the fullness, the content needs a container, and the lamp needs a lampstand. In the universe all things are of two sides. There is heaven and there is earth. There are men and there are women. There is the front and there is the back. There are the head and the body, the masters and the servants, the parents and the children, etc. Everything in the universe is always of two sides.

My point is this. The problem today is not with the Triune

God or with Christ. The problem today is with the church. The problem today is not with the Head but with the Body. With Christ as the divine, eternal, heavenly Husband, there is no problem. But what about the church as the wife? With Christ as the Head, there is no problem. But what about the church as the Body? There is no problem with the Triune God as the Dweller, but what about the church as the house? Even we have to ask, "Where is the house?"

If you read the Scripture thoroughly, from the beginning to the end, you will realize that the Triune God is trying His best to gain something for Himself. This is like gaining a man for the life, a wife for the husband, a house, a tabernacle, and a temple for the dweller, a city for the ruler, an army for the commander, a body for the head, the fullness for the reality, a vessel, a container, for the content, and a lampstand for the lamp with the light.

The first chapter of the Scripture deals with man and the second chapter deals with the wife. The section from the third chapter up to the beginning of the second book, Exodus, deals with the house. Then all the books from Exodus to the Chronicles deal with the tabernacle. The section from Chronicles to Malachi deals with the city, including the temple with the army. This covers the thirty-nine books of the Old Testament. If you want to understand the Old Testament, you need to have a thorough realization of these seven things: a man, a wife, a house, a tabernacle, a temple, an army, and a city. Then in the New Testament four things are dealt with: the Body of Christ, the fullness, the vessel, and the lampstand. Eventually, the seven items in the Old Testament plus the four items in the New Testament equal the New Jerusalem. This is the whole Scripture.

SATAN'S INTENTION

By going through the whole Bible in this way we can see what is in God's plan, God's economy, God's arrangement, God's administration. This is the very thing which the enemy of God hates so much. Throughout all the generations, the enemy has done and is still doing his best to frustrate, to damage, to spoil, and even to disrupt this very matter.

What Satan, the enemy of God, has always been doing is of two steps. First, if possible, he would hinder, frustrate, and prevent people from coming to the Lord Jesus to receive Him as their Savior. Next, if he could not do this, he will allow people to believe in Christ, but he will try to frustrate them from being built up together with others as the church.

The old enemy Satan considers the second matter more serious than the first. He knows God's intention in the whole universe is to have a house, a Body, a corporate container. As long as he can frustrate God from having His house, Satan is satisfied. Regardless of how much material and how many precious things there are, as long as the house is not there, it is all right with Satan. Look into the history of Christianity and the situation today; then you will realize what the enemy's intention is. The goal, the intention, of Satan is to spoil, to frustrate, and to hinder the building which God desires to accomplish.

GOD'S INTENTION

I have the full assurance that in these last days the Lord is doing something to recover the church life, the building of His Body, the building of His house. The present age is the age of the church, and God's aim, God's goal, is to have a church, to have a bride.

Many read the Gospel of John and realize that it says that Christ came that we may have life (3:16; 10:10b). But they do not know that this life is for the forming of the bride. John 3:29 mentions the bride. John the Baptist recommended the Lord not only as the Lamb of God (1:29) but also as the Bridegroom who has the bride (3:29). Christ came as the Lamb in order that He might obtain a bride.

We often say that Christ loved us and died on the cross for us. Galatians 2:20 does tell us that Christ, the Son of God, "loved me and gave Himself up for me." But do you know that there is also Ephesians 5:25, which says that Christ "loved the church and gave Himself up for her"? Christ gave Himself up not just for you but for the church. Christ loves you for the purpose of the church. His intention is to have the church.

We need to spend more time to learn about the twelve aspects of the church which we have pointed out. Learn to know the church as the universal new man with Christ as the appearance, form, and expression without and with Christ as the life within. Then learn to know the church as the wife, the counterpart of Christ. Learn to know the church as the wonderful house, the wonderful tabernacle, the wonderful temple, the wonderful city, and the army fighting for the kingdom and interest of God. Furthermore, you have to learn to know the church as the Body of Christ, the fullness of Christ, the corporate vessel, and the corporate lampstand. Eventually, you have to know the magnificent city, the New Jerusalem. If you desire to know Christ, you have to know these twelve items. Otherwise, you cannot know Christ in a full way.

THE PEARL OF GREAT VALUE

In this chapter my burden is to share with you about the church in another way. Do you know that the church in the eyes of the Lord is a pearl? As we have pointed out in the beginning of this chapter, the Lord likened the church to a pearl (Matt. 13:46). A pearl is something transformed in the death waters; it is not something created by God. This indicates that the church is not something natural; it was not there in God's creation. The church is something transformed in the death waters. The transformation of the church is something of life. Most of us know how a pearl is produced. Originally, a pearl was just a little rock or a grain of sand. One day an oyster is wounded by this little rock and it secretes its life-juice around the little rock. This secretion transforms the little rock into a wonderful pearl. This is also the story of how the church is produced. Christ came to the world which was filled with death, and He was wounded by the sinners. He secreted His life-juice around the sinners to make them into a pearl of great value, which is the church.

THE PARABLES IN MATTHEW 13

I wish to remind you of all the parables in Matthew 13. The first parable is the parable of the sower going out to sow the seed (vv. 3-8, 19-23). This sower is Christ Himself, who comes to sow His life as the seed into us.

The second parable is the parable of the tares, the false wheat (vv. 24-30). The Lord came to sow the good seed with the intention of getting the real wheat. But the enemy of the Lord came and sowed tares in the field; these tares grew up as the false wheat. This means that the Lord comes to give us His life with the intention of regenerating us as the true believers, the true Christians. But the enemy Satan comes to bring into existence on the earth a great number of false believers, false Christians. So not too long after the day of Pentecost, we see the wheat as well as the tares growing together in the field, that is, the true believers as well as the false believers existing together on this earth.

The third parable is the parable of the mustard seed (vv. 31-32). The mustard is an annual herb. It is small, lowly, and temporary, but good for food. However, its nature was changed so that it became a big tree. This indicates that the church must be an herb on this earth, small, lowly, temporary, full of life, and good for food. However, the nature of the church has changed. The church has become a big tree— Christianity. Look at the Vatican and St. Peter's Cathedral. What a tremendously big tree this is! When an herb becomes a tree, it is no longer good for food. It is good for the birds to lodge in. The birds in the first parable signify the evil one, Satan (vv. 4, 19), and the birds here refer to the evil persons, the sons of the devil, the false Christians, who lodge in today's Christianity as the biggest organization on this earth.

Where are you today? Are you in the little herb or in the worldwide, great tree? In the eyes of the world, as the church we should be nothing. We should be just like an herb, so small, lowly, and temporary on this earth, but really good for food. With the big tree, there is the vainglory of this age. If you want to do something for the church, you have to do it in a lowly way, in a small way. Do not try to do it in a big, tremendous way. Always keep in mind that the church is a small herb.

Then in the fourth parable we see a woman taking leaven and adding it into the meal, the flour (vv. 33-35). This woman, who is the same as the woman Jezebel mentioned in Revelation 2:20 and the great harlot mentioned in Revelation 17:1-5, signifies the Roman Catholic Church. This evil woman added leaven, signifying evil things (1 Cor. 5:6, 8) and evil teachings (Matt. 16:6, 11-12), into the fine flour, signifying all the teachings concerning Christ and, in particular, the truths concerning Christ as food. Leavened bread is easy to eat. The Roman Catholic Church put a lot of evil things into the truths concerning Christ to make them easy for people to take.

Do you know that Christmas is a kind of leaven? The birth of Christ is the meal, but Christmas is the leaven. In the Bible there is the birth of Christ but not Christmas. Christ was not born on December 25; He was probably born in the spring, not in winter. In ancient times people worshipped the sun as their god and celebrated December 25 as the birthday of the sun god. After the Roman Empire accepted Christianity, the people were unwilling to drop this celebration on December 25. So the Roman Catholic Church simply adopted this practice and told people that since Christ is the sun, December 25 is the birthday of Christ. Thus, they began the celebration of the so-called Christmas. The Catholic priests admit that Christmas is something false, but they also claim that it helps people to believe in the birth of Christ. This is an example of the "leaven" added into the truths concerning Christ.

Let me tell you a story as another example of the leaven added to the meal. Five years ago some of us went to Jerusalem for a visit. One day our tour guide took us to the Mount of Olives. He showed us a big rock on the top of that mountain and told us that it was the very spot where the Lord ascended. He also showed us a big footprint which is supposed to be the footprint of Jesus. After I revealed to him that I am a person who knows the Scriptures, he admitted that all the stories he told us were superstitions. Yet so many people from far away places would go there on Easter Sunday to kneel and kiss that footprint. This is the leaven added to the ascension of Christ as the meal.

A number of Catholic cathedrals have a statue of Jesus

placed at the entrance. The Catholics admit that that is not the real Jesus, but they say that it can remind people to receive Jesus. Again, this is the leaven mixed with the meal.

In the first four parables we see the line of the seed. The seed is of life and is good for food. In the first parable the seed is sown, in the second parable the seed grows up, in the third parable the seed grows up into something with its nature changed, and in the fourth parable something evil is mixed with the meal that comes out of the seed.

We may also say that with the first four parables there is the line of life. Christ came as the seed of life to be sown into us with the intention of growing something real. But at a certain point, there was a change in nature and consequently, there was a great change in appearance. Not only so, there was a corruption in element. The Lord came with the intention to sow Himself as the good seed of life, to grow as the true wheat, and to produce the pure meal. But the enemy came in to change the nature and appearance and to corrupt the element.

The fifth parable is that of the treasure hidden in the field (Matt. 13:44). The treasure must consist of gold and precious stones. Then in the sixth parable in Matthew 13:45-46, which we read at the beginning of this chapter, we have the pearl of great value. Both the treasure, consisting of gold and precious stones, and the pearl are not something created by God but are something transformed.

Here I wish to point out that, first, the church is produced out of Christ as life and, second, the church is produced out of the transformation of life. In the first four parables, the life is sown into us, and then in the fifth and sixth parables, there is the transformation of life. Now you can understand why in the New Jerusalem the city proper is of gold, the gates are of pearl, and the foundations of the wall and the wall itself are of precious stones (Rev. 21:18-21). This is what the Lord is seeking—a building of gold, pearls, and precious stones.

I look to the Lord that in these days He will grant you the grace that you may see the intention of the Lord, the desire of the Lord, and the goal of the Lord. If you want to practice the church life, you must have a clear understanding of all these parables concerning the church.

In summary, Christ as the seed of life is sown into us for the transformation of life. We have nothing to do with the big tree and the leaven. Today we are under the transformation of life to become gold, precious stones, and beautiful pearls as materials for God's building. The Lord sacrificed all that He was and all that He had to obtain the precious materials for His building. He gave Himself up to buy the pearl of great worth. So today it is worthwhile for us to sacrifice everything and pay the price to realize the church life.

1-1-95 C

we human beings are worthless until we get into the oyster.
the more we stay in Christ, the more valuable we become, not
because of us, but because of His element being added to us.

CHAPTER THREE

THE LIFE TO PRACTICE THE CHURCH LIFE

As we have mentioned in the previous chapter, the parables spoken by the Lord in Matthew 13 show us that the purpose, the intention, of the Lord in giving Himself to us as life is to bring forth the church as His Body. They also show us how the enemy has come in to frustrate the Lord's purpose by damaging, spoiling, and corrupting the Body of Christ. But praise the Lord, eventually, the church will be built up with gold, precious stones, and pearls through the transformation of life. Ultimately, there will be a city built with gold, precious stones, and pearls as the ultimate consummation of the people of God (Rev. 21:18-21).

OUR NEED FOR THE TRANSFORMATION IN LIFE

First Corinthians 3 tells us that the church is, on the one hand, God's cultivated land, and on the other hand, God's building (v. 9). On the one hand, we have to grow as God's farm by the life which is Christ Himself as the seed sown into us. On the other hand, we have to be transformed by this divine life into precious materials for the building up of the church. Then we will have the real church life.

Usually, when we talk about the practice of the church life or the practice of the Body life, immediately we begin to consider how to form or organize something according to our human thought. But we need to realize that the practice of the church life is not a matter of formation or organization. It is a matter of the growth in life and the transformation in life. Christ has to grow up in you, and you have to grow up in Christ. Moreover, we natural men have to be transformed into precious stones. If we try to form or organize a church, we are foolish. That means we have not learned from the history of the church and that we are going to repeat the past mistakes.

Our burden is not to teach people to be religious. What we need is to know Christ as the transforming life. Today the Lord is doing a hidden work of transformation in us. We do not need to be formed or organized, but we need to be transformed into precious materials for the building up of the Body of Christ.

You have been regenerated, so you have Christ Himself as the very life to grow in you and to transform you. You may know you have Christ in you as life, but how much have you been transformed by this divine life? I do not mean how much you have changed in your behavior. The Lord being life to us is for transforming us in our nature metabolically, not for changing or correcting our behavior outwardly. Hinduism, Buddhism, and Confucianism attempt to change the outward behavior, but the Lord's being life to us is to transform our inward nature.

You may have some changes in your behavior and some corrections in your actions due to some good, sound Christian teachings, but it is quite possible that you do not have any transformation accomplished within you. Corrections come from outward teachings, but transformation comes from the inner life. Suppose a certain brother is proud. After he hears a message telling him that pride is damaging, he receives the help and makes a decision to be humble. Perhaps he succeeds outwardly, but this is mere outward correction, an outward change in his behavior. This is not the transformation in life.

What is the transformation in life? May the Lord open our eyes so that we can see that Christ is life in us. Regardless of how good or how bad we are, we have been put to death, terminated, crucified. Today it is Christ who lives in us (Gal. 2:20). As genuine Christians, we do not need to correct our conduct or adjust our behavior. We need to see that Christ is our life and that we have been crucified with Christ. One day we will pass through such a crisis, and we will see such a vision. Then we will seek to experience Christ in our practical daily life, not just to know Christ in doctrine. We will seek and pray, "Lord, let me know the practical way to take You as life in my daily life." When we know the way to take Christ as life, day by day we will be filled with Christ, occupied with Christ, and saturated with Christ. We will be persons full of Christ.

What is the practical way to take Christ as life? The most important thing is for us to realize that Christ today within us is the law of life (Heb. 8:10; Rom. 8:2) and the anointing (1 John 2:20, 27). To have the doctrinal teaching that Christ has sown Himself into us to be the life in us is not sufficient. Look at our daily life. By what life do we live? By Christ or by ourselves? Does the fact that Christ is life within us and that we have been put on the cross have any influence on us? Is there always a checking of the cross in our daily life—in whatever we say, whatever we do, and wherever we go? The problem is that we know the fact, but we still live by ourselves.

The building of the church absolutely depends on the transformation in life. We have to be transformed. If you take Christ as your life practically in your daily life and are checked by the cross all the time, you will have a different view concerning the church life. Your view will be changed. You need to put this into practice. Then you will know where you are, and you will know the real church life. If you are still living by yourself, your view concerning the church will be natural. When you deny yourself to take Christ as your life and are willing to be checked by the cross in all your daily affairs, your view about the church life will be changed and even revolutionized because you are being transformed.

The more we talk about the doctrine, the more we will be in darkness about the church life; our inner eyes will be veiled. But if we are willing to be checked by the cross all day long in all things and to take Christ as life in every matter, our eyes will be opened and the veils will be gone. Then we will see the church, the Body of Christ, and the church life, the Body life.

GOING TO THE LORD IN PRAYER
FOR HIS ENLIGHTENMENT

Brothers and sisters, the church life needs the real growth

in life and the transformation by the life of Christ. I do not feel that I need to talk a lot about how Christ is life to us. But I do have the burden to give you a challenge. Do you live by Christ or by yourself today? You need to go to the Lord and have a genuine and thorough prayer before Him. Just pray for one thing: "Lord, do I take You as my life day by day? Do I live by You?" Also, how much room in your life has been given to the cross? How much ground does the cross have in you? Do you really mean it when you say that "it is no longer I who live, but it is Christ who lives in me" (Gal. 2:20)?

I believe that if we go to the Lord and pray in such a way, we will be exposed in the light of the Lord and will find out that even up to now we are still very natural. We have very little transformation. We know that Christ is life to us, but day by day we do not live by Christ. Moreover, we are not learning the lessons of the cross. We do not always take the cross as a check to our daily life. We have the knowledge in our mentality, but we do not have the practice in our daily life.

If you take the cross and are checked by the cross, you will realize that Christ is so living and real within you. He is not only active but also acting. Because He is living, you will sense something acting, enlightening, anointing, regulating, ruling, and governing within you. There is something within you, and that is Christ in a practical way.

In this chapter I am giving you a simple secret. You need to pray about this matter today. Pray to Him in a real and thorough way, saying, "Lord, I am here. I have been a Christian for many years, but I wish to know where I am and how I am. Put me in Your presence and in Your light. Expose me and let me see where I am. Lord, do I really mean it when I say that You are my life? Do I have some experience of the cross by applying it to my daily life? Do I have some transformation?" I urge you to go to the Lord and pray in this way. Then you will see where you are.

Forget about taking care of your behavior. More than thirty years ago I was a young learner in the service of the Lord. At that time I did only one thing: I was always careful about my work, my attitude, and my actions. I tried to be very careful in these matters. Many times I went to the elderly saints and asked them in a humble way, "Have I done something wrong in these days? Would you be kind enough to let me know? Please tell me."

In those early days I spent much time with Brother Watchman Nee. Many times I went to him asking him to tell me something about my condition. He just smiled and never said anything. Later, the Lord revealed to me that when I was so concerned about my behavior, my attitude, and my work, it proved that I was so much in myself. One day the Lord opened my eyes to see that I needed to forget everything about myself and learn the lesson of being checked by the cross. The problem today in the church life is the natural life. The natural life has to be put away, eliminated, and Christ must be everything.

I say again that if you would go to the Lord and pray in this way, I have the assurance that you will sense how real, how living, how active, how positive, and how illuminating Christ is within you. You will have the living Christ, the acting Christ, and the anointing Christ operating within you experientially all the time. Then you will learn how to forget about yourself and to live and walk by taking Christ as your life. Eventually, you will have a transformation in life and not just some correction or adjustment in your behavior. Your whole being with your very nature, element, essence, and substance will be transformed by Christ in a living and real way. In this way you will realize the church life in a way which is absolutely different from the past.

CHAPTER FOUR

WHAT CHRIST IS

Christ is the life and reality of the church. Now we need to know the right way, even the best way, for us to apply and experience Christ as life to us. However, before we get into this matter, we need to find out what Christ is. If we want to apply Christ as life to our experience in our daily life, we need to know what kind of Christ He is. Of course, it is impossible to know Christ in a thorough way. We can never exhaust the knowledge of Christ because He is all-inclusive and His riches are unsearchable (Eph. 3:8). Nevertheless, we have to try our best to know what He is.

THE NEED TO KNOW CHRIST
WITH THE CHURCH

At the end of the first chapter, we pointed out that in Ezekiel 1 there is a big wheel moving all the time on the earth (vv. 15-21). If you consider this matter in the light of the whole Scripture, you will realize that this wheel is the move of God in the universe. This wheel as the means by which God acts and moves in this universe must be Christ with the church. Christ is the center, the hub, and the church is the circumference, the rim. If we want to practice the church life, the Body life, we need to know the church and where the church is in God's economy. Even more, we need to know what Christ is. Christ and the church are the great mystery in the universe (Eph. 5:32). Where the church is, there is Christ, and where Christ is, there is the church. You can never separate Christ from the church. Whenever we speak about the church, we must know what Christ is and how He is related to the church.

CHRIST BEING THE MIGHTY GOD

We all know that Christ has many names, and I believe that among these many names the first must be *the Son of God*. Then we have to ask, "Who is the Son?" Let us read Isaiah 9:6: "For a child is born to us, / A son is given to us; / And the government / Is upon His shoulders; / And His name will be called / Wonderful Counselor, / Mighty God, / Eternal Father, / Prince of Peace." The little child is the Mighty God. This is the difference between the very God in whom we believe and the God in whom the Jewish people believe. The Jewish people believe the only God, who is the Mighty God, but they do not believe that this Mighty God became a child.

CHRIST BEING BOTH THE SON AND THE FATHER

Then there is another name—*the Eternal Father*. He is the Son, yet He is called the Eternal Father. Some people try to argue by saying that the Son is called the Father, but the Son is not the Father. I cannot understand how the Son can be called the Father yet not be the Father. It is foolish to say that a person is called John Clark, yet he is not John Clark. If the Son is called the Father, He must be the Father. If He is not the Father, how can He be called the Father? The clear and definite prophecy in Isaiah 9:6 tells us that the very child born in the manger in Bethlehem is the Mighty God and that the Son given to us is the Eternal Father. A Son is given, yet His name is called the Eternal Father. The very Son who has been given to us is the very Father.

This is confirmed by John 14:8-11. Now let us read this portion carefully: "Philip said to Him, Lord, show us the Father and it is sufficient for us. Jesus said to him, Have I been so long a time with you, and you have not known Me, Philip? He who has seen Me has seen the Father; how is it that you say, Show us the Father? Do you not believe that I am in the Father and the Father is in Me? The words that I say to you I do not speak from Myself, but the Father who abides in Me does His works. Believe Me that I am in the Father and the Father is in Me; but if not, believe because of the works themselves." Here again we see that the Son and the Father are one. Some would say, "How could the Son pray to the Father if the Son is the Father?" This is not a problem. Andrew Murray once said that the best prayer is the Christ who dwells in us praying to the Christ who is in heaven.

CHRIST BEING THE SPIRIT

Now let us turn to the third chapter of 2 Corinthians. In this chapter the apostle Paul revealed that everything today in the New Testament is a matter of the Spirit. Then in verse 17 he said, "The Lord is the Spirit." This means that the Spirit mentioned in the preceding verses is the Lord Himself. The Lord here refers to Christ the Son (2 Cor. 4:5). The Lord as the Son is called the Father, and He is also the Spirit. First Corinthians 15:45b says, "The last Adam became a life-giving Spirit." The last Adam, no doubt, refers to Christ in the flesh. Can you say that this Spirit is different from the Holy Spirit? It is not logical to say this. We have to admit that this Spirit whom Christ is, is the very Holy Spirit. Thus, it is clear that the Lord, who is Christ the Son, is the Spirit also.

In John 14:8-11 the Lord told us clearly that He and the Father are one and that He is in the Father and the Father is in Him. Now in verses 16 through 19 He told us that He and the Spirit are one. In verses 16 through 17 He said, "And I will ask the Father, and He will give you another Comforter, that He may be with you forever, even the Spirit of reality, whom the world cannot receive, because it does not behold Him or know Him; but you know Him, because He abides with you and shall be in you." In these two verses, referring to the Spirit, the Lord used the pronoun "He." But in verse 18 He changed the pronoun to "I," saying, "I will not leave you as orphans; I am coming to you." By this we realize that the very "He" who is the Spirit of reality in verse 17 is the very "I" who is the Lord Himself in verse 18. "He" is "I" and "I" is "He." Then verse 19 says, "Yet a little while and the world beholds Me no longer, but you behold Me; because I live, you also shall live." This refers to the time of resurrection. After His resurrection, the Lord came back to the disciples. He left them for no more than seventy-two hours, or three days. Hence, it was only "a little while." Then the Lord came back, and the world could no longer see Him, because He became the Spirit. Yet we believers can see Him because He is within us as the Spirit. In John 14 we see that the Son and the Father are one and that the Son and the Spirit are also one. The Son is the Father, and the Son is also the Spirit. Thus, there are the Father, the Son, and the Spirit, but They are one God.

CHRIST BEING THE TRIUNE GOD

Some may ask, "What is the meaning of having three persons since They are one God?" Let us read 2 Corinthians 13:14. "The grace of the Lord Jesus Christ and the love of God and the fellowship of the Holy Spirit be with you all." In this verse we have three things: love, grace, and fellowship; we also have three persons: God, Christ, and the Holy Spirit. We have to realize that these three are one. Love, which is in the heart, is the source; grace is the expression of love; and fellowship is the transmission of grace. By grace, love is expressed, and by fellowship, grace is transmitted. These are not three different matters, but three forms of one thing. In the Father it is love, with the Son it is grace, and by the Holy Spirit it is fellowship. What is imparted to us through the fellowship of the Spirit is the grace of Christ, and what is expressed through the grace of Christ is the love of God.

Ice, water, and vapor are not three different kinds of substances, but one substance in three forms. In our hymnal, we have this line: "What mystery, the Father, Son, and Spirit,/ In person three, in substance all are one" (*Hymns,* #608, stanza one). There is one God in three persons, yet His substance is one. We must never have the thought that the Son is separate from the Father and that the Son is separate from the Spirit. The Son is the embodiment of the Father, and the Son is the Spirit.

Some teach that the Holy Spirit is separate from Christ or that the Holy Spirit is a kind of power given to us by Christ. This is wrong. The Holy Spirit is Christ Himself. In eternity past, in the heavens, unapproachable to men, God was the Father. When He came to the earth to manifest Himself to mankind, He was the Son. And today, when He comes into us to dwell in us and mingle Himself with us, He is the Spirit. He is the Father as the source, the Son as the expression, and the Spirit as the transmission, the fellowship. The Father, Son, and Spirit are not three separate Gods. The Son is the Father, and the Son is the Spirit. This is the Triune God.

Let us read Romans 8:9-11. Verse 9 says: "But you are not in the flesh, but in the spirit, if indeed the Spirit of God dwells in you. Yet if anyone does not have the Spirit of Christ, he is not of Him." In this verse, Paul first spoke of *the Spirit of God* and then he changed and referred to *the Spirit of Christ*. This shows that the Spirit of God is the Spirit of Christ. They are not two Spirits; They are one Spirit. Then in verse 10, Paul changed again and used the title *Christ,* saying, "But if Christ is in you, though the body is dead because of sin, the spirit is life because of righteousness." Then in verse 11, he changed again from *Christ* to *the Spirit,* saying, "And if the Spirit of the One who raised Jesus from the dead dwells in you, He who raised Christ Jesus from the dead will also give life to your mortal bodies through His Spirit who indwells you." Hence, in these three verses we have the Spirit of God, the Spirit of Christ, God Himself, and Christ Himself. They are not four separate persons; these are four titles of the one Lord, the one God. The Spirit of God is the Spirit of Christ, the Spirit of Christ is Christ, and Christ is God.

I am stressing this because we have to know what kind of Christ we have. The Christ we have and in whom we believe is the Triune God. Also, Christ is the center of the Triune God. He is the Son with the Father as the Spirit. Within Him is the Father and He is the Spirit. If you have Him you have the Father, and if you have Him you have the Spirit. Therefore, if you want to know Him, you have to know the Spirit, because the Father is in the Son and the Son is the Spirit. Also, if you want to know the Son with the Father, you have to know the Spirit.

It is the greatest mystery in the whole universe that God, Christ, and the Holy Spirit are one, and no human mind can fathom it. However, we have to accept this great mystery according to what the Scripture speaks about it. We should not exercise our limited mind to understand it merely as a doctrine of theology. We have to exercise our inspired spirit to realize it as the divine fact and experience the three persons of the Divine Trinity for our enjoyment. The Divine Trinity is not mentioned in the Scripture as a point of theology for us to study; it is unveiled to us in the Scripture as a divine reality for us to partake of, experience, and enjoy.

CHRIST BEING A MAN

The Son is the center with the Father in Him, and He is the Spirit. But there is something more. He is the Son of Man. One day He became a man. In His incarnation the Triune God, the Father in the Son as the Spirit, mingled Himself with man (John 1:14). Jesus the Nazarene, the man, is the very God. Do you believe this? If you do not believe this, you are not a Christian, but a Jew or a Muslim. The Jews and the Muslims believe God as the Creator, but they do not believe that God has ever been incarnated as a man. But we believe. If anyone does not believe this but claims that he is a Christian, he is an anti-Christ Christian. All sound, proper, and genuine Christians believe that this Triune God is a man, a God-man, a Triune God-man, the Triune God mingled with man.

When I was young, I had a wrong concept about the Lord. I thought that in His incarnation He put on man as a piece of clothing for thirty-three and a half years and that after His death and resurrection He put off the clothing which He had put on. Later, I realized that this is wrong. Christ is still a man today. After His resurrection, He came to His disciples with His physical body. Of course, that body was something wonderful which we cannot understand in a full way. It was a resurrected body, a spiritual body, yet it was physical. He showed the disciples His hands and His feet and asked them to touch Him because He had flesh and bones (Luke 24:39-40). Hence, after His resurrection, He is still a man.

Now let us read Matthew 26:63-64. "But Jesus remained

silent. And the high priest said to Him, I charge You to swear by the living God to tell us if You are the Christ, the Son of God. Jesus said to him, You have said rightly. Nevertheless I say to you, From now on you will see the Son of Man sitting at the right hand of Power and coming on the clouds of heaven." The high priest asked the Lord if He was the Son of God, but He answered with "the Son of Man." After His ascension to the heavens, the Lord is still the Son of Man, and even when He comes back on the clouds of heaven, He will still be the Son of Man. He is not only the Triune God but also a man.

Now let us read Acts 7:55-56. "But being full of the Holy Spirit, he [Stephen] looked intently into heaven and saw the glory of God and Jesus standing at the right hand of God; and he said, Behold, I see the heavens opened up and the Son of Man standing at the right hand of God." This shows clearly that even after His ascension, the Lord Jesus today is in the heavens as a man. Furthermore, 1 Timothy 2:5 says, "For there is one God and one Mediator of God and men, the man Christ Jesus." The Lord Jesus is and will be forever a man. He is the Triune God mingled with man, so He is the God-man, the Triune God-man. He is the complete God and the perfect man with His divinity and His humanity. He was incarnated with a specific purpose—to enter into humanity and put humanity on Himself as one of the main parts of His person today, and He will keep humanity for eternity. He will be man as well as God forever and ever.

CHRIST AS EVERYTHING

Therefore, what is Christ? Christ is the Son with the Father as the Spirit mingled together with man. In Christ are the Son, the Father, the Spirit, and the man. All the fullness of the Godhead dwells in Him (Col. 2:9). All the fullness of the Father is in the Son, all that the Son has is in the Spirit, and all that the Spirit has is in the man. This is the very Christ in whom we believe, and this is the very Christ who dwells in us. This is the Savior in whom we believe, the Lord whom we serve, and the very God whom we worship. This is the Christ who is life to us. In this life we have the Father, the Son, the Spirit, and the man.

Here is a cup of plain water. Later, you add in some lemon juice. Then it is no longer just water, but water mingled with lemon juice. Before His incarnation, God was merely God. But after His incarnation, He is God mingled with man. Within Him is the human nature, the human essence, the human element in addition to His divinity. With our Christ there are both divinity and humanity, both the divine element and the human element. He is not only the Triune God but also *the* man. He is the Father, the Son, and the Spirit—the Triune God—and the man. He is everything. As God, He is the Creator, and as a man, He is a creature (Col. 1:15). So in Him we have the Creator and the creature.

But this is not all. It is wonderful that we can never exhaust telling what He is. Besides being the Creator and a creature, He passed through human living on this earth for thirty-three and a half years. Then He suffered death and conquered death. He passed through death and He came out of death. Thus, in Him there is the element of the effectiveness of His all-inclusive death. Although death is an awful thing, the death of Christ is a great blessing, a great deliverance, and a great release to us. The death brought in by Adam sent us into hell, but the death of Christ brings us out of hell. The death brought in by Adam was a real trouble to us, but the death accomplished and passed through by Christ is a real deliverance to us. We have to sing much about the death of Christ. We have to shout, even proclaim, that we have the death of Christ.

Moreover, the death of Christ is the killing power, the killing element. Today in some doses of medicine there is an element that kills the germs in your body and an element that nourishes your body. In Christ we have the killing power and the nourishing supply. The killing power is the element of the effectiveness of His death, and the supply is the resurrection life. Death kills, but resurrection supplies. Death solves the problems, but resurrection supplies us with the rich provision of life.

After resurrection, there is the ascension of Christ. Now

He is in the heavens and He is transcendent. In this transcendency He is enthroned with authority and glorified. With Christ there is also the kingdom. We simply cannot exhaust all the items of Christ. In this one great "dose" we have the Creator, the creature, the human nature, the human living, the effective death, the resurrection, the ascension, the enthronement, the glorification, and the kingdom. This great dose is Christ Himself. The Christ who is life to us is such an all-inclusive Christ, and He is so much. He is the Son of God, the Father, the Spirit, and the man. Everything is with Him and in Him. We have to know Christ in such a full way. When we take Christ as our life day by day, we will experience Him in all of these aspects.

I hope that we would bring all these things to the Lord and pray much that the Lord, the Spirit, may reveal them to us, not just in the way of knowledge but in the way of revelation and vision, that we may see the rich reality of Christ in whom we believe and whom we serve. We have to know what kind of Christ we are experiencing as life day by day and how we can contact, experience, partake of, and enjoy such a Christ.

CHAPTER FIVE

EXPERIENCING CHRIST
AS THE INNER LIFE

LIGHT, THE SPIRIT, FELLOWSHIP, JOY,
THE LAW OF THE SPIRIT, AND PEACE
BEING RELATED TO LIFE

Let us read John 1:4: "In Him was life, and the life was the light of men." Here we have the life and the light. We are also told that the life is the light. This life which is the light is the Word who is God Himself (1:1). In God Himself, the living Word, is the life, and this life is the light. Therefore, light is related to life.

John 6:63 says, "It is the Spirit who gives life; the flesh profits nothing; the words which I have spoken to you are spirit and are life." Here life is related to the Spirit, and the Spirit who is life is also the Word. The life with the Word is related to the Spirit.

First John 1:1-4 says, "That which was from the beginning, which we have heard, which we have seen with our eyes, which we beheld and our hands handled, concerning the Word of life (and the life was manifested, and we have seen and testify and report to you the eternal life, which was with the Father and was manifested to us); that which we have seen and heard we report also to you that you also may have fellowship with us, and indeed our fellowship is with the Father and with His Son Jesus Christ. And these things we write that our joy may be made full." Here we see two more things that are related to life—fellowship and joy. Therefore, light is related to life, the Spirit is related to life, fellowship is related to life, and joy is related to life.

Verses 5 through 7 say, "And this is the message which we have heard from Him and announce to you, that God is light and in Him is no darkness at all. If we say that we have fellowship with Him and yet walk in the darkness, we lie and are not practicing the truth; but if we walk in the light as He is in the light, we have fellowship with one another, and the blood of Jesus His Son cleanses us from every sin." In these verses we see again that light is related to life.

We also need to read Romans 8:2: "For the law of the Spirit of life has freed me in Christ Jesus from the law of sin and of death." Here we are told that the Spirit is the Spirit of life, and with this Spirit of life there is a law. Of course, the law of the Spirit of life is related to life. Then verse 6 says, "For the mind set on the flesh is death, but the mind set on the spirit is life and peace." Peace is also related to life.

In the above passages of Scripture there are at least six things that are related to life: light, the Spirit, fellowship, joy, the law of the Spirit, and peace. The burden in my heart in these days is to help the Lord's children know the proper way to experience Christ as life. In other words, my real burden is to help people know the way of the inner life. Christ is living within us today to be life to us, but how can we experience Christ as life all the time?

GOD'S INTENTION FOR US TO PUT ASIDE OUR NATURAL LIFE AND TAKE CHRIST AS OUR LIFE

Before we go on to see the way, I feel that I need to share a little concerning the matter of God's intention. Although we have a physical life, a natural life, a human life by birth, God's intention is that we take Christ as our life. This is something quite "troublesome." We have a life already, yet God wants us to take another life. We are so used to living by the natural life which we already have, yet today God wants us to give up, to put away, to put aside, this natural life and take Christ as our life.

Many Christians do not know that there is the need of a change of life, not a change of their behavior or conduct. We have to put our natural life aside and take another life. However, the natural thought or concept is always to improve, correct, or even repair the natural life just like repairing a poor, old car. God's demand, however, is that we put the car away and take an airplane. We may have a 1921 Ford, a poor little old car, and our intention is to repair it, to change some of its parts to improve it, and to paint it and make it look nicer. But God wants us to put it away and take the airplane.

The problem is that we are so used to the poor car and have developed some affection for it, so we are not willing to put it aside. Perhaps we put it aside, but we still go back to look at it. This is our story. What we are doing all the time is trying to repair the "poor car" to improve it a little. But God demands that we forget about the old car, the poor car; that is, forget about our old self, our own life. God wants us to put that life aside and take Christ who is the heavenly airplane. We need to take Him as our life.

In the past years I have seen thousands of Christians, even good Christians, in the Far East, in Europe, and in this country. But very few practice this matter of day by day putting away the "old car" and taking the "airplane." They are good and religious Christians, but they are not living by Christ or taking Christ as their life.

In 1937 the church arranged for me to stay in a Christian home. The couple and their family were so good. Day by day I had the realization that both the husband and wife were nice and wonderful, but I was concerned that they did not know how to put themselves away and take Christ as their life. I could sense that they were good, naturally and religiously, but they were not taking Christ as their life. They talked with me about a lot of things and about a lot of persons, but what was their standard? Their standard was not Christ, but good and evil. They knew how to be good and how not to be evil, but regretfully, they did not know how to take Christ as their life. They often remarked that a certain kind of conduct was not Christ-like. They knew how to be Christ-like, but they did not know how to take Christ as their life.

Do you realize that there is a difference between being Christ-like and taking Christ as your life? You may be Christ-like, but you may not know at all what it means to take Christ as your life. From my own experience I know it is easy for me to preach the gospel to a very evil person, but it is rather hard for me to preach the gospel to a good person. I learned that I had to be careful and patient in trying to preach the gospel to a good person. I might say something like this: "In the garden of Eden, the tree of the knowledge of good and evil was in contrast to the tree of life. Good is not life, just as evil is not life. Only Christ Himself is life. God does not want us to be good or evil. God wants you and me to take Christ as our life." Brothers and sisters, we have to put away, to put aside, our natural life and take Christ as our life.

THE WAY TO TAKE CHRIST AS LIFE

What is the way to take Christ as life? You have to be clear about several things before you can be clear about the way to take Christ as your life. First, you have to realize that today Christ is the Spirit (2 Cor. 3:17; 1 Cor. 15:45b). Many Christians have the impression that the Holy Spirit is absolutely someone other than Christ. In fact, they have the impression that the Holy Spirit is just the power, the strength, of Christ. But the Holy Bible says that the Father is in the Son and the Son is the Spirit.

Today we have the Father in us (Eph. 4:6), Christ in us (2 Cor. 13:5), and the Holy Spirit in us (Rom. 8:9). So do we have three in us or one in us? Actually, the three-one God is in us. I was very young when I got saved, and the more I prayed to the Lord in heaven, the more I felt that He was within me. When I was young, I went to some elderly brothers and asked, "When we pray, what do we call Him? Do we call Him Lord or Father?" Some said it is better to call Him Father, others said it is better to call Him Lord, and still others said it is better to call Him Lord God the Father. Actually, They are one. The Father is in the Son, and the Son is the Spirit.

Second Corinthians 3:17 says, "The Lord is the Spirit." First Corinthians 15:45b says, "The last Adam became a life-giving Spirit." By these two verses we can realize that Christ is the Spirit. Furthermore, 1 Corinthians 6:17 tells us that "he who is joined to the Lord is one spirit." If Christ is not the Spirit, how can we be one spirit with Him? This very Spirit who is the Holy Spirit of God is now in our spirit to mingle with our spirit as one spirit. If we are going to take Christ as life, we have to know that Christ today is the Spirit and this Spirit is now mingled with our spirit as one spirit.

He who is joined to the Lord is one spirit, and the Spirit Himself witnesses with our spirit (Rom. 8:16). These two spirits, the divine Spirit and our human spirit, cooperate together, work together, and mingle together as one spirit. The entire matter of taking Christ as our life hinges on the wonderful Spirit who is in our spirit. This is something wonderful that is beyond our comprehension. But what we are seeing here is something real and revealed in the Scripture. It is so wonderful that we have a wonderful mingled spirit, a spirit which is the mingling of the divine Spirit with the human spirit, the mingling of divinity with humanity.

We also must realize that the Spirit is life. The Lord told us that the words He speaks to us are spirit and are life (John 6:63). The Spirit is life, and Christ Himself is life. But how do you know that you have this Spirit as life within you? If you have this life within you, which is Christ Himself and also the Spirit of life, you have the fellowship of life. The current of electricity is a good illustration of the fellowship of life. When the electricity is working, there is the current of electricity. This electrical current is simply the electricity itself flowing. If you have the current of electricity, that means you have electricity itself flowing and working. What is the fellowship of the Holy Spirit? What is the fellowship of life? That is the current, the flowing, of life within you.

We can also use blood as an illustration. We have blood within us and the circulation of blood. What is the circulation of blood? It is the blood itself circulating, flowing. If you have blood without circulation, that means you are dead. How do you know you are living? Because something is circulating, flowing, in you. How do you know that you have Christ as the Spirit within you as life? Because you have something within you flowing all the time. There is a current within. A stream, a current, is flowing within you. This is the fellowship.

If you do not have this flowing within, you are a dead person; you are a false Christian, not a genuine one. If you are a genuine Christian, I am sure something within you is flowing all the time. That is fellowship. The fellowship of life is the current of the Spirit. In 2 Corinthians 13:14 we have the love of God, the grace of Christ, and the fellowship of the Holy Spirit. The fellowship of the Spirit is the current of the Spirit, transmitting all the fullness of God to us. This is just like the current of electricity. While it flows, it transmits all the riches of the generator to the building. The Holy Spirit is the fellowship, the transmission, transmitting all the riches of Christ, all the fullness of the Godhead in Christ, into us.

How do you take Christ as your life? You have something within flowing in you; just take care of that flowing, follow that flowing, and go along with that flowing. If you follow and go along with the inner flowing, this means that you are on the right track to experience Christ as life day by day. When the inner flowing tells you to go to Los Angeles, do not say, "I don't want to go." Instead, go along with the inner flowing and do whatever it tells you to do. To take Christ as life is to go along with the inner flowing.

Not many people know this secret of taking Christ as life. Some may know yet they are not faithful to the inner flowing. Many times something in you is flowing, yet you do not go along with the flowing. You try to be good and do good in order to make yourself Christ-like, but you would not go along with the flowing to take Christ as life. This is the problem.

If you go along with the inner flowing, you will have joy. Joy is very much related to the flowing, the fellowship. If the flowing tells you to go to Los Angeles and you go along with it, you will be full of joy. A Christian must be a person who is always joyful, but you cannot be joyful unless you go along with the inner flowing. The joy is always with the flow.

How do you know that you are taking Christ as your life? Just ask yourself, "Do I have joy?" This is something that you cannot pretend. Some brothers came to me pretending to be joyful, but in my spirit I could sense their joy was false. Joy is something from within your spirit. If you have the flow and are in the fellowship, you have joy and are joyful. If you neglect the inner flow, the inner fellowship, you lose your joy. Remember that joy is always related to fellowship.

Now let us consider the next item—the light. The life was the light of men (John 1:4). In John 8:12 we have this term *the light of life*. The light of life is just life itself. The light within us is life, and the life within us is the light. Light is something shining, illuminating. Check your experience. Do you have something within you shining all the time? If you do, that means you are in the life. How do you know that you are taking Christ as your life? By realizing, sensing, that you have something within you not only flowing but also shining. I have no utterance to describe this inner shining, just as I have no way to describe the taste of sweetness. If you want to know what sweetness is, just take a piece of candy and taste it. Then you will know.

I believe many times you have the experience of the shining within you. That is the light of life, the life functioning as light. We know that electricity is one, but its functions are many. It gives us light, power, heat, etc. Just as there is one electricity yet many functions, there is one life yet many functions. It gives us the flow, the joy, and the light. Something within us is shining all the time. If you sense darkness within you, you should realize that you are not taking Christ as life; you are out of the experience of Christ as life. If you take Christ as life, you must have the shining within you because the life is the light, and Christ Himself is the light of life.

Let me share a little testimony with you. Just before I came here this evening, around suppertime, I was with the Lord considering the message tonight. I had prepared a message which was different from what I am speaking now. I had everything ready for that message, but I sensed a darkness in me. Somehow I was in a shadow. Then when I was with the Lord, the sense came to me that I had to give the message which I am speaking here tonight. I said to the Lord, "Lord, no doubt, I will go along with You." Right away within me it was transparent. The cloud was lifted and the sky became clear.

How do you know that you are going along with the Lord? Just by checking in this way, "Am I clear? Or am I cloudy, smoggy, foggy?" If you have the cloud, the smog, or the fog, that means there is something between you and the Lord. You are on the wrong track. You need to be adjusted within. Some brothers like to make jokes. I would ask you, "After you make a joke, do you feel you are clear within? Or do you sense you are foggy, smoggy?" There is nothing wrong with your morality when you make jokes, but if you are a person who jokes too much, I am sure you are a person not taking Christ as life. If you are one who takes Christ all the time as life, you will not joke, because the life of Christ is not a joking life. Joking is unbecoming to the inner life. I use this illustration to show you how you can know whether you are in the flow or not, whether you are in the transparent spirit or under the clouds. When you take Christ as your life, you have joy, and you have the shining.

Now let us consider the law of life within us. The life is the law. With any kind of life, in principle, there is a law. The divine life, which is Christ Himself, is the very law. Christ within you is not just the life, the light, the fellowship, and the joy, but also the law. You have an inner, living regulating. You have some regulations within you, not written in word but written in the Spirit. The inner regulating of this life is deep, strict, and fine.

You know what is right and what is wrong; you know what you should do and what you should not do. You know because you have the regulating within you. Since I learned the lesson of the inner law of life, I realize one thing—there is no need for you and me to tell people what is right and what is wrong, what to do and what not to do. Whenever a saint comes to me and asks me something about good or evil, right or wrong, I always answer him by asking, "How do you feel?" You know the answer. There is a living rule within you, and this living rule is Christ Himself. He is not only the life, the light, and the flow; He is also the law.

In the Old Testament times God gave Moses the Ten

Commandments as the law. That law is the description, the definition, of God. By that law we know what kind of God He is. But today in the New Testament times, God Himself comes into us as the law. The old law of letters consisted of words written as the description of God. Today God Himself comes into us as the living law. This is something subjective, something inside of us; it is not something objective, something outside of us. The Lord Himself, the living One, is the law within us. What kind of relationship should you have with Him? It is not according to the regulations of the so-called church or according to doctrinal teachings, but according to the inner regulating.

In the Old Testament times, an Israelite could do a lot of good things, and he could even sacrifice himself and all that he had for others. In spite of all the good things that he had done, if he did something against the law, he still had a problem before God. Today it is the same with us related to the law of life. If we are not right with the inner regulating, no matter how many good things we may have done, we know there is a problem within between us and God. Maybe we would preach the gospel, minister the word, and do a lot of things to help others, but we know there is a problem between us and God because we are wrong with the inner regulating.

One time a brother was going to do a certain work for the Lord, yet he realized that the inner regulating was demanding him to stop the work. However, he had the intention and the desire to do it. He argued with the Lord, saying, "Lord, that work is so good and so helpful to others, and it is also profitable for You. Besides if I do it, the church will be helped a lot." But no matter how much he argued with the Lord, the more he went to do it, the more he lost the inner peace. The more he went to work on that project, the more he lost the inner anointing. He did a lot of good things, but he was wrong with the Lord.

Today we maintain a proper relationship with God not by doing good things but by going along with the inner regulating. You need to take care of the inner anointing. How do you know you are taking Christ as life? If you are really taking care of the inner anointing, you will go along with it even if it stops you from doing good things such as sacrificing yourself to love others. You should not argue with the Lord that this is something good, something for Him, or something for His people. The Lord just wants you to take care of the inner anointing and regulating.

You need to take Christ as life by taking care of the inner regulating. If you do not go along with the inner regulating, you are not a person taking Christ as life all the time. Christ as life is in you as the living law regulating you. In all things He is the law; you are not the law. He is the rule; you are not the rule. He is the living rule, the living law, always regulating you from within.

Then there is also the matter of peace. Romans 8:6 tells us that "the mind set on the spirit is life and peace." How do you know that you are taking Christ as life? By the sense of peace in you. Everything within you and every part of your being is peaceful, restful, and at ease. When you are taking Christ as life, when you are in the light, in the flow, and under the regulating, you have the wonderful, perfect peace. This is not an outward peace but an inward peace. This is the peace in the heart, in the spirit, and even in the soul—in the mind, emotion, and will. You have the whole peace, the perfect peace, the heavenly peace, the divine peace within you.

How do you know you are taking Christ as life? Just by checking if you have the fellowship, the joy, the shining, the regulating, and the peace all the time. Many Christians neglect their inner life. They work, walk, and have their being on their own and according to their moral standard. To them, as long as they are not doing something evil, it is good enough. They do not take care of Christ within them. Brothers and sisters, we should not be such poor Christians. We have to take care of the inner life all the time. Today Christ is the living One (Rev. 1:18) within us as life.

Thus, we have the flow, the joy, the light, the law, and the peace. We have the living One within us flowing, shining, and regulating. This means that we are in Christ, taking Christ as life, living by Him, and consequently, having the image of Christ expressed in our daily walk. When we have

Christ within as our life, surely we will have the expression of Christ without.

The way to take Christ as life is to take care of the inner sense, the inner registration, and to check if you have the inner flowing, the inner shining, the inner regulating, and the inner joy with the inner peace. If you have all these inner things, you are in Christ taking Him as your life. If not, you are outside of the experience of Christ as life. Furthermore, no matter how good you are apparently and outwardly, you still need to check with your inner sense. You are in Christ taking Him as life only when you have the inner flowing, shining, and regulating with joy and peace. This is the right way for us to experience Christ as life.

Very few Christians are living in the inner life, but many Christians are living in an outward way. We have to be Christians in the inner life, always learning to take Christ as our life. We need to forget about ourselves and take Christ as our life by checking to see that we have the inner flowing, shining, regulating, joy, and peace.   1-22-95 C

Only 2 ways: human way, or divine
- Try to fix it
- facts: the Lord is the Spirit
- the Christian life is in my spirit!

If the source of your good behavior is the Spirit, and not your trying to fix yourself, then there are certain indicators:
- fellowship
- light
- peace
- law of the spirit of life.

When we try to fix it up, we don't have the sense of these 4 matters.

We go back to the old life because:
- we are used to it
- we appreciate it.

Spend time with Him in the light!
- we will see we appreciate that old good human source
- we will put it aside
- " " live by the divine life within!

Our spirit is the key!
Constantly check where we are at!

CHAPTER SIX

WHAT IS THE SPIRIT?

THE SPIRIT OF THE GLORIFIED JESUS

John 7:37-39 says, "Now on the last day, the great day of the feast, Jesus stood and cried out, saying, If anyone thirsts, let him come to Me and drink. He who believes into Me, as the Scripture said, out of his innermost being shall flow rivers of living water. But this He said concerning the Spirit, whom those who believed into Him were about to receive; for the Spirit was not yet, because Jesus had not yet been glorified."

When the Lord was speaking this word to His disciples, the Spirit of God was already there. Yet the Spirit at that time was not yet, because Jesus had not yet been glorified. What does this mean? To find out the meaning, we have to know when He was glorified. Many of us think that the Lord was glorified when He was taken into the heavens. But this is not accurate. Luke 24:26 shows that by His resurrection the Lord was glorified. That verse says, "Was it not necessary for the Christ to suffer these things and enter into His glory?" This word was spoken before the Lord was taken up to the heavens. After His resurrection, He met the two disciples and told them that He had entered into glory already. Thus, it was by resurrection that the Lord was glorified.

What does it mean for the Lord to be glorified? The Lord is the God of glory (Acts 7:2; 1 Cor. 2:8). One day He was incarnated to be a man. The very God of glory came into a man and put man upon Himself. He concealed all the glory of God within this man. Thus, the glory of God was covered, veiled, by this man. When He was on this earth, people just saw Him as an ordinary man. Outwardly, He was merely a humble man, yet inwardly, He was the God of glory.

Eventually, He passed through death and was resurrected.

By His resurrection He was glorified. We can use a grain of wheat or a seed of any kind of beautiful flower as an illustration. Within the seed, the glory of the flower is concealed, veiled. Once the seed falls into the earth and grows up and blossoms, that is its glorification. The Lord died and resurrected. Through His resurrection the very glory of God which had been concealed, veiled, covered, in His flesh was manifested. This was His glorification.

When the Lord was on the earth, the Spirit was not yet, because the Lord had not yet been glorified (John 7:39). It was after the Lord's glorification, that is, after His resurrection, that the Spirit entered into His disciples. After the Lord resurrected, He came in the evening to the disciples and breathed into them, saying, "Receive the Holy Spirit" (20:19-22). This shows clearly that the Holy Spirit came into the disciples after the Lord had been glorified in His resurrection.

THE SPIRIT OF JESUS

Now let us read Acts 16:7: "And when they had come to Mysia, they tried to go into Bithynia, yet the Spirit of Jesus did not allow them." *The Spirit of Jesus* is a special term. This is not the Spirit of God and not even the Spirit of Christ, but the Spirit of Jesus as a man. Now let us read the previous verse. Verse 6 says, "And they passed through the region of Phrygia and Galatia, having been forbidden by the Holy Spirit to speak the word in Asia." The Spirit of Jesus in verse 7 is the Holy Spirit in verse 6. After the Lord's resurrection, the Holy Spirit is the Spirit of Jesus.

THE SPIRIT OF JESUS CHRIST

Philippians 1:19 says, "For I know that for me this will turn out to salvation through your petition and the bountiful supply of the Spirit of Jesus Christ." Here it is not just the Spirit of Jesus but the Spirit of Jesus Christ. The Greek word for *bountiful supply* is a special word used by the Greeks when they referred to the supplying of all the needs of the chorus by the choragus, the leader of the chorus. In ancient times, according to the Greek custom, the leader, the choragus, of the chorus had to prepare and supply everything that the chorus needed. Now the apostle Paul used the same word to describe the bountiful supply of the Spirit of Jesus Christ.

THE SPIRIT OF CHRIST

Romans 8:9 says, "But you are not in the flesh, but in the spirit, if indeed the Spirit of God dwells in you. Yet if anyone does not have the Spirit of Christ, he is not of Him." This verse interchangeably uses the Spirit of God and the Spirit of Christ. The Spirit of Christ is the Spirit of God. They are one Spirit.

THE SPIRIT OF GOD IN THE OLD TESTAMENT AND THE SPIRIT IN THE NEW TESTAMENT

If we want to know what the Spirit is, we first have to distinguish the Spirit of God in the Old Testament from the Spirit in the New Testament. In the fifth chapter of his book *The Spirit of Christ,* Andrew Murray told us that in the whole Old Testament there is not such a title as *the Holy Spirit.* In the entire Old Testament you cannot find the title *the Holy Spirit* ascribed to the Spirit of God. (In Psalm 51:11 and Isaiah 63:10-11, *Holy Spirit* should be translated *Spirit of holiness.*)

The title *the Holy Spirit* was used first in connection with the preparation for the Lord's coming through incarnation (Luke 1:15, 35). It was at that time that the holy Scripture used the term *the Holy Spirit* for the Spirit of God. Hence, this title *the Holy Spirit* is related to the fact that God mingled Himself with man through incarnation. Such a mingling cannot be found in the Old Testament.

The Old Testament mentions a number of times that the Spirit of God, or the Spirit of Jehovah, came down upon the prophets or upon a certain person (Judg. 3:10; 6:34; 11:29; 13:25; 14:6, 19; 15:14; 1 Sam. 10:6; 16:13-14; 2 Sam. 23:2; 1 Kings 18:12; 22:24; 2 Kings 2:16; 2 Chron. 18:23; 20:14; Isa. 11:2; 63:14; Ezek. 11:5; 37:1; Micah 3:8; Zech. 7:12). Thus, in the Old Testament there was God, and there was the Spirit of God who came down upon people. At that time the Spirit of God had merely the element of divinity.

We know that God passed through a wonderful process in the New Testament. He became a man in incarnation, and His divinity was mingled with humanity. Then He passed through human living, crucifixion, and resurrection. In resurrection He was glorified and became the life-giving Spirit (1 Cor. 15:45b). This Spirit is all-inclusive. How many items are in this Spirit? The Son is in this Spirit, the Father is in this Spirit, and, of course, the Spirit is in this Spirit. The man whom Christ became through incarnation is in this Spirit. His human living, the effectiveness of His death, His resurrection, glorification, ascension, enthronement, kingdom, and authority are all included in this Spirit. Such a Spirit is the Spirit of Jesus (Acts 16:7), the Spirit of Christ (Rom. 8:9), and the Spirit of Jesus Christ (Phil. 1:19). In the Old Testament, the Spirit of God had merely the element of divinity. But today all the elements of God, man, human living, death, resurrection, glorification, ascension, enthronement, and the kingdom with the authority are in the Spirit. We have the bountiful supply of the Spirit of Jesus Christ.

THE EXPERIENCE OF THE ALL-INCLUSIVE SPIRIT

Sometimes when you experience the Spirit working and moving in you, you sense some kind of killing going on within you, even though you may not have heard any message or teaching about the killing of the cross. Because you experience the Spirit of Jesus working in you, you sense something within killing your poor character, your bad habits, your temper, your desires, your lusts, and a lot of other things. This is the effectiveness of the death of Christ included in the Spirit of Jesus. This is like a dose of medicine with many elements, including the element of germ-killing. Once this dose gets into you, it kills the germs in your body. There is no need to remember the messages about the killing power of the cross. As long as I have the Spirit working and moving in me, I sense the killing. The more I am filled by the Spirit, the more I will be killed, because within the Spirit of Jesus there is the killing element, the effectiveness of Christ's death.

Sometimes when the Spirit is moving within you, you have

the sense that the Lord is on the throne and that you have to be prostrate before Him as the Lord of all. The more you have the Spirit moving within you, the more you will be subdued by Christ. You will recognize the lordship and headship of Christ.

Also, as the Spirit is moving within you, many times you have the sense that you are transcendent. The more you have the Spirit moving within you, the more you have the sense that you are not on this earth but in the heavenlies. You are far above all. It seems as if nothing can touch you. All things are under your feet.

At other times when the Spirit is moving within you, you will have a sense that you have to be so humble and lowly. This is something of Christ's human living. No one who has the Holy Spirit moving within him can be proud. The more you think highly of yourself, the more it proves that you are out of the Holy Spirit. If you are in the Spirit and have the Spirit moving within you, you will be a humble person. If you have the Spirit moving within you, on the one hand, you are transcendent, high in the heavenlies, and on the other hand, you are lowly and humble.

Furthermore, the more you are filled with the Holy Spirit, the more you will be human. Many people claim that they are spiritual, yet they do not act as men. They try to act like angels, who are spirits (Heb. 1:13-14). God's intention, however, is not to have many spirits, but many men filled with the Spirit. If a certain brother has never wept in the meeting, he is not human. The Gospel of John tells us that the Lord Jesus is the Son of God (3:16), the very God (1:1). Yet this same book tells us that He wept (11:35), that He was weary and needed to rest (4:6), that He was hungry and sent His disciples to get some food for Him (vv. 8, 31), and that He was thirsty and asked the Samaritan woman for some water to drink (v. 7). The Lord is the very infinite God, yet today He is also a man with the human nature.

I have seen some so-called spiritual persons who never laugh or weep. They say, "If we are in Christ, we shouldn't weep or laugh. We have to be very strict." I am not trying to help you to be more emotional or sentimental. But I do know that a person who is spiritual must be very human. The Spirit of Jesus today has not only the divine element but also the human element. I would recommend to you the book *The Spirit of Christ* by Andrew Murray. You should pay special attention to the fifth chapter. In this chapter he said that the divine nature had been interwoven into the human nature. Today, this interweaving of the divine nature and the human nature is in the Holy Spirit. Today we use the word *mingling* (as used in Leviticus 2:4-5 in the type of the meal offering) instead of the word *interweaving*. According to the type of the meal offering, the Lord Jesus was the fine flour (humanity) mingled with oil (divinity). Today with the Spirit of Jesus there is a mingling of divinity with humanity. If you are properly experiencing the Spirit of Jesus, you will be very human in a pure way according to a high standard.

In the Spirit there is also the strength to bear all kinds of sufferings. While the Lord was on this earth, He was suffering all the time. The suffering element, the suffering strength, the suffering capacity, is now in the Spirit of Jesus. When you have the Spirit moving within you, you will sense there is the strength, the ability, the capacity, to endure sufferings. When you are filled with Him, you are able to bear all things and endure all things. This is divinity mingled with humanity.

Not only so, many times when we are in the Spirit, we sense something within us as the resurrection power, which is living, energizing, strengthening, and powerful. The greater the depression, suppression, or even oppression, the greater will be the energizing, the standing up, and the rising up within you. This is the resurrection power. You may not have known that the resurrection life of Christ is within you today, but if you have the experience of the Spirit of Christ, you have the element of the resurrection power that is in Him.

One time some of us brothers were invited to a certain brother's house for dinner. While we were there, the brothers, including the host, were talking excitedly about their reading of the book of Romans, and I was listening to their talk. After quite a while, I asked them what kind of light they had received. One brother said that they had really seen something in Romans 6 about reckoning oneself dead. I smiled and said, "Brother, would you tell me frankly and faithfully if you are really dead by your reckoning?" He said, "Brother Lee, I have to confess that the more I reckon myself to be dead, the more I am alive."

Then by the help of the Spirit, I pointed out to the brothers that it is not by reckoning that we become dead. We have to be in the Spirit. What is mentioned in Romans 6 must be realized in Romans 8. If you have Romans 6 without Romans 8, it is like having a book on electricity without electricity. It may be a good book about electricity with many instructions and formulas, but it is not the electricity itself. The "electricity," that is, the Spirit of life, the Spirit of Christ, is in Romans 8. We need the Spirit of Christ.

From 1925 up to 1932, I tried and tried to reckon myself to be dead. But the more I reckoned, the more I was living. Then one day the Lord opened my eyes to see that in the Spirit of Jesus there is the effectiveness of death. In this big "dose" there is the killing power. Simply take the dose. Forget about the formula, the teaching, the doctrine. Simply take the Spirit with the killing element. The more you take the dose, the more you have the killing power. The more you experience the Spirit, the more you have the killing element. All the riches, all the reality, all the fullness of what Christ is, what Christ does, and what Christ has, are in this very Spirit. We do not need the teaching, the knowledge, about Christ. We need the very experience of the Spirit of Jesus Christ.

Why was it that in Acts 16 when the apostle Paul would try to go to a certain place to preach the gospel, the Spirit of Jesus did not allow him? Why does the Scripture say "the Spirit of Jesus" instead of "the Spirit of God" (v. 7)? There must be some reason. When we look into Acts 16 and see the environment of that chapter, we realize we need the Spirit of Jesus. In this chapter there is much suffering and persecution. Paul was even put into prison! In such a situation the Spirit of Jesus was really required. Paul needed the Spirit of Jesus, the Spirit of a man with abundant strength for suffering.

We often have a wrong concept about the apostles. In Acts 14 we are told that a great crowd in Lystra thought that Paul and Barnabas were two gods (vv. 11-13). But in Acts 16 we see they were not gods but men who had the Spirit of Jesus. In this chapter the apostle Paul suffered much persecution and eventually was put into prison.

I do not have the utterance to adequately express what I apprehend in my spirit about this matter. But one thing I can say is that the more you are filled with the Spirit of Jesus, the more you will be nothing on this earth. You will be finished. Jesus was not a great man in the world's eyes. He was just a lowly carpenter. He was human. He laughed, He wept, He drank, He ate, and He cared for people. Furthermore, He suffered. Many times there was no deliverance for Him. You should not have the thought that since you are so spiritual, you will be delivered from many troublesome matters. Actually, the more spiritual you are, the more troubles you will have.

Brothers and sisters, today within you there is such a wonderful, all-inclusive Spirit. This Spirit is the Spirit of reality (John 16:13). He is the reality of the Son, the Father, the Spirit, and the man Jesus. He is the reality of Christ's human living, death, resurrection, glorification, ascension, enthronement, kingdom, and authority. All these things are made real in the Spirit. If you have this Spirit, you have all these things. If you do not have the Spirit, you have nothing but mere doctrinal knowledge in your mentality. Only the Spirit can give you the reality because He Himself is the reality (1 John 5:6b). If you have Him, you have the reality and experience of all these wonderful things.

Let us pay our full attention to the Spirit who is the reality of every positive thing in the universe and who is now in us. Then we will have the wonderful experiences of Christ. This is what we need today.

1-29-95C

CHAPTER SEVEN

THE LAW OF THE SPIRIT OF LIFE

THE LIVING LAW WITHIN US

Hebrews 8:10-11 says, "For this is the covenant which I will covenant with the house of Israel after those days, says the Lord: I will impart My laws into their mind, and on their hearts I will inscribe them; and I will be God to them, and they will be a people to Me. And they shall by no means each teach his fellow citizen and each his brother, saying, Know the Lord; for all will know Me from the little one to the great one among them." Notice in verse 10 that *laws* in the plural number is used. But in the original passage in Jeremiah *law* is used. Jeremiah 31:33 says, "I will put My law within them." Later, we will see why "law" eventually becomes "laws."

Romans 8:2 speaks of "the law of the Spirit of life." Three things are composed together here: the law, the Spirit, and life. The law is of the Spirit, the Spirit is of life, and this life is Christ Himself, who is God. This verse goes on to tell us that the law of the Spirit of life is in Christ Jesus and has freed us "from the law of sin and of death."

Verse 9 says, "But you are not in the flesh, but in the spirit, if indeed the Spirit of God dwells in you. Yet if anyone does not have the Spirit of Christ, he is not of Him." We have previously pointed out that the Spirit of God and the Spirit of Christ in this one verse are not two Spirits. They are just one Spirit. The Spirit of God is the Spirit of Christ, and the Spirit of Christ is simply Christ Himself, because verse 10 says, "But if Christ is in you, though the body is dead because of sin, the spirit is life because of righteousness."

In the previous chapter, we saw what a wonderful, all-inclusive Spirit we have within us today. In this chapter we will see that this Spirit within us is a law. When I say "the law of the Spirit of life," please do not think of it as three things, the law, the Spirit, and the life. Actually, the life is the Spirit and the Spirit is the law.

Suppose you had a hamburger for lunch today. The hamburger was made up of different ingredients such as bread, beef, lettuce, onion, pickles, and mustard. Therefore, the lunch, the hamburger, and all the ingredients were not many different things. They were just one thing. Similarly, when we speak of the law of the Spirit of life, we should realize that the law, the Spirit, and the life are not three things but just one thing.

In John 6:63 the Lord Jesus said, "It is the Spirit who gives life...the words which I have spoken to you are spirit and are life." First, the Lord indicated that for giving life He would become the Spirit. Then He said that the words He speaks are spirit and life. We know the word is the Lord Himself, and the Lord Himself is life. So the Lord, the Spirit, the word, and the life are just one thing.

Now how can we say that the law is the Spirit and that the law is the life? Let me illustrate in this way. In the Old Testament, God gave His people the Ten Commandments as the law. This law is a description, a definition, and an explanation of what God is. The Ten Commandments can be summarized into four main points. They reveal to us that God is holiness, righteousness, love, and light. The complete law reveals to us the nature and character of God, showing us what kind of God He is.

People in the Old Testament had to deal with all the items of the law. If they were wrong with any item of the law, that meant they were wrong with God. They had to get right with God according to the Ten Commandments. They had to do everything according to the holiness, righteousness, love, and light of God. Then they would be right with God.

Today, however, it is different. God Himself comes into us in the Son as the Spirit to be the living law within us. Suppose your father wrote you a lot of regulations when he was away from you. But now he comes to stay with you. He himself becomes the living regulation to you. Even more so, in the

New Testament under the new covenant, God puts Himself into us as the living law. When God comes into us, He is the living law within us.

We have seen that Christ in us is our life and the light of life. We have something shining within us, enlightening us. This life is also the law, so we have something regulating within us. When we have Christ, we have something living, shining, and regulating within us. This is the acting, working, and moving of the Lord Jesus as life within us. I am burdened for the children of God to have a clear vision about this matter. The Lord has to take away all the veils and open this mystery to us that we may see this wonderful One.

LIVING ACCORDING TO THE INNER LAW OF LIFE

I am concerned that many of you may be very good, yet you are wrong with the Spirit. You may work for God today, preach the gospel, do a lot of things to build up the churches, and even give what you have to help others. But I would ask you, "Are you right with the Spirit in you?" One day when the Lord comes back, He will not ask you about so many things. He is concerned about only one thing, that is, whether or not you are right with Him according to the inner law of life.

Today it is not a matter of work or doing. It is a matter of how you deal with the living One who dwells in you. Are you right with Him? I say again, you may be very good, very religious, and seemingly very spiritual, but I am afraid you are not in the Spirit. According to your actions, your expressions, your doings, and your speaking, you are altogether outside of the Spirit. You are not right with the Spirit. You are not right with the inner law. You do not take care of the inner regulating, but neglect it all the time.

In Revelation 2, the Lord told the church in Ephesus, "I know your works and your labor and your endurance and that you cannot bear evil men; and you have tried those who call themselves apostles and are not, and have found them to be false; and you have endurance and have borne all things because of My name and have not grown weary. But I have one thing against you, that you have left your first love"

(vv. 2-4). As a wife, you may do a lot of good things for your husband, but are you right with your husband? Do you have a genuine love for him? This is the problem.

We are talking about the Christian life and the church life. What is the Christian life? What is the church life? The Christian life is not a religious life; it is a life which is Christ Himself lived out through us. We must take Christ as life and live by Him day by day. We need to love Him and be willing to be regulated, governed, and ruled by Him. Then we will be walking in this living One, and we will be in the reality of the Christian life. The church life is not something organized or something regulated by teaching. The church life is Christ lived out through us in a corporate way. You live Christ and I live Christ, and this very Christ unites us together in oneness. Then together we have the corporate life of Christ expressed.

The church life is not produced by a lot of discussion. This is the way of the United Nations in New York or of the United States Congress. This is not the church life. Strictly speaking, in the church, there is no need of discussion. If we need a lot of discussion, that means we are fallen; we are wrong. If you take Christ as everything, all the problems will be solved, settled, through the cross.

Brothers and sisters, I am very much concerned about this matter. We may know how to be religious, but we do not know adequately how to take Christ as our life that Christ Himself may be lived out through us. We may know the forms and the teachings, but do we know the real church life which is Christ Himself lived out through us in a corporate way? We need to be definite and subjective. This wonderful Christ is living, acting, and moving within us. He is shining on us and regulating us all the time. The only need is for us to take care of this inner regulating.

Sometimes brothers or sisters would come to me and ask me about certain things, but I had something within holding me back from speaking. According to the inner regulating, I could not say anything. If we learn to forget about all the outward things and simply take care of the inner regulating, we will have a wonderful church life. The church life is Christ Himself.

Even though we love the Lord, we still act apart from Him most of the time. In our daily living and walk, we are like Peter before the Lord's resurrection. Before the Lord's resurrection, Peter was one who loved the Lord. Yet he acted on his own all the time. He was a good brother, but he acted by himself. At that time he did not live by Christ, walk in the Spirit, and take Christ as life, strength, and power for his service to God. Like Peter, we may seem to love the Lord so much, but we do not take Him as our life in our daily living. Most of the time we walk and act either according to our own opinions, thoughts, and ideas or according to religious doctrines or church concepts. What the Lord wants is that we take Him as our life and walk in oneness with Him by fellowshipping with Him all day long.

Sometimes after I finished reading the Holy Bible, I had to confess to the Lord and ask for His forgiveness. This is because while I was reading it, the Lord was demanding that I pray. But I was not willing to pray at that moment because what I was reading was really interesting. Therefore, I would go on with my reading and ignore the inner regulating. Outwardly, it seemed that I was nicely reading the Word, but inwardly I was disobedient to the Lord. Hence, the Christian life is not an outward matter but an inward matter. This is why in the New Testament we are taught not to judge people according to their outward actions. A person may be very good, right, and religious, yet he may be very disobedient to the Lord within. He does things always according to his own taste and preference. He has his desire, his intention, and his motives, but he does not know the meaning of the cross.

We have to humble ourselves before the Lord, confessing to Him, "Lord, maybe I am not sinful or worldly, but I am disobedient to You. Maybe people would appreciate and applaud me, thinking that I am religious, right, and good, yet they don't know that I disobey You all the time. I don't take You as my life. I don't walk in You or live by You. I don't know the meaning of the cross and the meaning of walking in the Spirit. I don't know the law of the Spirit of life in me." Then we need to go further and pray, "Lord, I need Your deliverance. Deliver me from things other than Yourself. You are the living One. You are the only One who is living, acting, moving, working, shining, and regulating within me all the time. Lord, help me to take care of You and to go along with You. Help me to forget about all the outward things." We need to humble ourselves before the Lord in this way.

The life for the practice of the church life is Christ Himself experienced by us through the cross. We must be put to death by the cross. This should not be merely a doctrine. It must be our experience. In our daily life, we should always deny ourselves and take Christ as our life. Then we will have the church life.

Without the cross on the negative side and the living Christ on the positive side, we will have many problems whenever we come together. Each one of us is a problem. If we are not willing to be put away by the cross and to take Christ as our life, we will be a problem. Do not listen to this message for others. Do not nod your head, saying, "This message is good for Brother So-and-so. I am glad he is here." If you say this, this simply shows that you are in yourself and out of Christ. If you are in Christ, you will say, "Lord, this is what I need. I need this for Your Body, the church. I need this for the practice of the church life. I need the cross. I need You as the living Christ. I need to know You as the living One within me. I need to know how You regulate me and shine in me. I need to go along with You in me."

Brothers and sisters, when we learn the lesson of the cross and experience Christ as the living One and the law of the Spirit of life in us, we have the church life. The church life is nothing less than Christ Himself lived out through us in a corporate way.

CHAPTER EIGHT

THE CENTRAL THOUGHT OF GOD

Scripture Reading: Rev. 1:4; 3:1; 4:5; Eph. 2:15-16, 19; Col. 3:10; Eph. 4:22

The point which we are going to cover in this chapter is more important than all the other points covered in the previous chapters. I would ask you to exercise not only the understanding of your mind but also the apprehending ability of your spirit, so that the Holy Spirit may reveal to you something eternal.

OUR HUMAN, RELIGIOUS CONCEPT VERSUS WHAT THE NEW TESTAMENT TEACHES

Before I touch the main subject, I wish to say something about our human, religious concept. This concept may be described in the following way. God is our Creator. He is holy, righteous, good, and loving, so we have to worship Him. However, we realize that we are sinful and that we need to repent and confess our sins before Him. We also realize that He loved us and even sent His only begotten Son into this world to be a man. This man, Jesus, died on the cross for our sins. Then He resurrected and ascended to the heavens, and now He is sitting at the right hand of God to be our High Priest, our Advocate, interceding for us all the time. If we believe in Him, put our trust in Him, by His redemption our sins will be forgiven and we will be saved. We will be reconciled to God, justified by God, and accepted by God. Then God will be favorable toward us. From this time on, we will enjoy His favor, and He will always be good to us. If we are weak, He will help us. If we have some troubles, He will take care of them. We can pray to Him about all our needs. Furthermore, we have to try our best to please Him, to serve

Him, and to glorify Him. This describes many people's religious concept. All these things are right and are up to the standard of our human concept, but they are not up to the standard of the divine revelation, the standard of God's purpose and desire.

Have you noticed that in our human concept there is nothing that pertains to the matter of life? In our concept there is nothing concerning Christ coming into us to be our life. This is a big shortage, a serious shortage. It is not enough just to have the sound, scriptural, fundamental Christian teachings. We must see that what the New Testament teaches is that Christ comes into us to mingle Himself with us. When we say "Christ," we mean the all-inclusive One who includes many wonderful items such as the Divine Trinity, divinity, humanity, human living, death, resurrection, glorification, ascension, enthronement, the kingdom, and the authority. All these things today are embodied in Christ as the wonderful Spirit.

Today this wonderful, all-inclusive Spirit is in our spirit (Rom. 8:16; 1 Cor. 6:17). We have everything in our spirit! This is something in the center of God's thought, yet it is neglected by Christianity. Many Christians consider the Holy Spirit as merely a power, a force, or a sensation coming down upon us to give us some gifts, might, strength, and power, and to help us to do good and serve God. They do not realize that the Spirit of God today is the all-inclusive and bountiful Spirit of Jesus Christ within us (Phil. 1:19b).

TRANSFORMATION BY THE SPIRIT

This wonderful Spirit who is Christ Himself is going to transform us absolutely into Christ with Christ. I would use a simple illustration. Suppose I have a white cotton ball, and I want to make it a red cotton ball. What should I do? I have to fill the very heart, the very center, of the ball with red ink. Then the red ink will gradually permeate and saturate the ball, and the ball will gradually absorb the red ink until it loses its white color and expresses something red. This means that the cotton ball, having been completely saturated and permeated by the red ink, is transformed into the red ink with the red ink.

You are the "ball," and this wonderful Spirit of Christ, who is Christ Himself, is the "red ink." At the time you received Christ, this wonderful Spirit came into you, into your spirit and heart, the center of your being. Now His intention is to permeate and saturate you with Himself so that you may absorb Him. By receiving Him and absorbing Him, your whole being, including all your inward parts, will be renewed, permeated, and saturated with Him and be transformed into Him. Eventually, your whole being will be full of Christ, mingled with Christ. Then you will lose your natural color and have the spiritual color, the "Christ" color. This is the central thought of God, and this is what God is seeking today.

We need a heavenly vision to see this matter in an adequate, concrete, and full way. We need to see and know that God's purpose, God's intention, is to have the all-inclusive Spirit of Christ come into us as everything that He may permeate us, saturate us, and transform us into Christ with Christ. This is not just a change of our behavior or living. This is a transformation of our nature.

Sanctification involves not only a change in position, that is, a separation from a worldly position to a position for God, as illustrated in Matthew 23:17, 19 and in 1 Timothy 4:3-5; it involves also a transformation in disposition, that is, a transformation from the natural disposition to a spiritual one by Christ as the life-giving Spirit saturating all the inward parts of our being with God's nature of holiness. This is what is mentioned in Romans 12:2 and 2 Corinthians 3:18. We have been sanctified in position, but we still need to be sanctified in our nature, in our disposition. This means that we need to be permeated and saturated by the Spirit so that we may be transformed into Christ with Christ. Then we will be absolutely and practically a part of Christ. As parts of Christ, we are members of Christ's Body.

TRANSFORMATION FOR THE BODY LIFE

Suppose we have two brothers—one American and one Chinese. On the one hand, I would say they are members of the Body of Christ because they are two genuine believers. They have been born again and are children of God. But on the other hand, it is hard to see that they are members of Christ because the Chinese brother is still very Chinese and the American brother is too American. Can something Chinese or American be in the Body of Christ? Colossians 3:11 tells us that in the Body "there cannot be Greek and Jew"; there cannot be any natural person. We should not bring anything Chinese or American into the Body of Christ.

In the Body there is no Greek, no Jew, no Chinese, no Japanese, no American, no Frenchman, no Englishman, no German, no Mexican, and no Puerto Rican. In the Body there is room only for Christ. If the Chinese brother remains Chinese and the American brother remains American, they are not members of Christ in actuality. They may have a little "red ink," a small measure of Christ, in their heart, but they have not yet been saturated by Christ. If you are saturated by Christ, you are in Christ and have been swallowed up by Christ to express Christ.

Some have asked me, "By what way do you run your church?" I said, "By the way of Christ." In Ephesians 4 we are told to put off the old man and to put on the new man (vv. 22, 24). What is the new man? The new man is the Body, and the Body is Christ (1 Cor. 12:12). We have to put on Christ, but first we have to put off the old man. We have to put off being Chinese or American. We have to realize that we were buried at the time of our baptism (Rom. 6:3-4). We have been terminated, we are finished, and we are through! The Americans are through and the Chinese are through. In the Body of Christ, there is no American, Chinese, British, and German; there is no old man. There is only the new man, who is Christ Himself.

The subject of this book is the life and way for the practice of the church life. Christ Himself is the life, and He is the Spirit in us. Today the Body life, the church life, is Christ Himself realized as the Spirit and dwelling in us. The only thing you need is to realize that you have this wonderful Spirit within you as the reality of Christ, as the fullness of the Godhead, and as everything to you. Furthermore, you have to renounce yourself. Renounce both your evil things and good things, both your failures and successes. Renounce your whole being. Forget about yourself.

You have Christ as the Spirit in you. He is moving, acting, living, working, shining, regulating, and anointing within you. You need to follow this wonderful Spirit and cooperate with Him, go along with Him, and take Him as everything for yourself. Moreover, you need to learn the lesson of renouncing yourself. You can never practice the church life by the human life. If you do not learn the lesson of remaining on the cross all the time, there will be a lot of trouble in your practice of the church life. Every brother and sister is a problem. Human nature is troublesome. All of us have to go to the cross. If there are "you and I," there is no Body, no church. This is why Paul said, "I am crucified with Christ; and it is no longer I...but...Christ..." (Gal. 2:20a).

We all have to see that the practice of the church life is not by bringing everyone into agreement with one another through discussions, talks, and negotiations with certain terms or conditions. Rather, the way to practice the church life is to put everyone and everything on the cross and to have everyone take Christ as life. Then we will be permeated and saturated by Christ and with Christ. Then we will be from within to without, wholly, thoroughly, and absolutely a member of Christ.

The Body of Christ is the new man created in Christ (Eph. 2:15). Do you think the creation of the new man has been accomplished? On the one hand, it has been accomplished, but on the other hand, it is in the process of being accomplished. Day by day we are under the process of transformation, permeation, and saturation. We have to see that God desires to transform our whole being, that is, to permeate our whole person with Christ. It is not merely a religious change, improvement, correction, or adjustment. It is absolutely a transformation with Christ, by Christ, and into Christ.

THE LAW OF LIFE SATURATING OUR INWARD PARTS

We need to be transformed by Christ and saturated with the wonderful Spirit. This is why the one law in Jeremiah

31:33 has become many laws in Hebrews 8:10. There are many laws because we have many parts, our inward parts. Jeremiah 31:33 says, "This is the covenant that I will make with the house of Israel after those days, saith Jehovah: I will put my law in their inward parts" (ASV). One law is put into many parts.

The term *inward parts* is also mentioned in Psalm 51:6, which says, "Behold, You delight in truth in the inward parts." Our inward parts are the parts of our soul—the mind, emotion, and will. We have the mind to think, the emotion to love, and the will to make decisions; all these parts need to be saturated with Christ. God put His one law into us. This one law is the law of the Spirit of life (Rom. 8:2). The law is the Spirit and the Spirit is the life. God put Himself into us as the all-inclusive Spirit, who is a law. This law saturates our emotion, subdues our will, and renews our mind. This one law regulates us, rules us, controls us. We do not need outward teachings. We have an inner regulating, which is illuminating, energizing, and strengthening. Thus, the one law put into us becomes the many laws in our inward parts. Actually, there are not many laws, but one law with many functions. It is the same with the one Spirit of God who is referred to as the seven Spirits in the book of Revelation (1:4; 3:1; 4:5; 5:6). The one Spirit is the all-inclusive Spirit, the sevenfold Spirit, with many functions for many purposes. Seven is the number that represents completion and perfection. The Spirit of God is complete, perfect, and all-inclusive. It is one Spirit with many all-inclusive functions.

If we remain on the cross and go along with the wonderful, indwelling, all-inclusive Spirit with His many functions, we will become a real part of Christ and will automatically, spontaneously, happily, gladly, and enjoyably have the church life. We will have the reality of the church, the Body of Christ. There is no need for any kind of organization, because we are a living organism of Christ.

I hope that we all can see the central thought of God as revealed in the Scripture. I do believe this is what the Lord is going to recover in these last days, that is, the knowledge, the realization, and the apprehension of the wonderful Spirit transforming, working, subduing, illuminating, anointing, and regulating within us all the time. The Lord is working in this country to recover the genuine church life, not the church organization, forms, formalities, rituals, charters, regulations, and rules. The time is ripe now, and people everywhere in this country are really seeking. They are seeking Christ as life and the church as the living expression of Christ.

I do have the assurance in these days that the Lord is going to recover the experience of Christ as life and the way to practice the church life so that Christ may have a living expression through His Body in many localities. This is the unique burden with which the Lord has burdened us.

2-12-95C

If you touch the Lord in your spirit there is no more me.

Realize: you have the wonderful Spirit in you

Renounce: yourself.

CHAPTER NINE

TRANSFORMATION BY THE SPIRIT

Scripture Reading: Rom. 8:2, 6, 16, 29; 12:1-2, 4-5; 2 Cor. 3:17-18

OUR NEED TO SET OUR MIND ON THE SPIRIT

In this chapter we want to fellowship about our need to be transformed by the Spirit. Within our spirit we have the wonderful all-inclusive Spirit, but without we have something awfully troublesome. This is our natural man, the man of the flesh. Outwardly, people may look nice, but actually no one is nice. Everyone is troublesome. We have this wonderful One within us, but we still have the old man, the old nature, the flesh, and the soulish life.

We have two realms from which to choose: the realm of the spirit and the realm of the flesh. Now the crucial thing is what we do with our mind. Our mind may be a mind of the flesh, or it may be a mind of the spirit. The mind represents the man. Whether we stand with the spirit or with the flesh depends on the attitude of our mind. The mind set on the flesh is death, and the mind set on the spirit is life and peace (Rom. 8:6). What is the attitude of our mind today? Is it set upon the spirit or the flesh?

In the garden of Eden there were three items: the tree of life, the tree of knowledge, and a man standing before the two trees (Gen. 2:8-9). Do you realize that within you today there are these three things? First, you have the spirit, the divine Spirit mingled with your human spirit, with all the wonderful things of God. Second, you have the flesh with something of Satan. Third, you have the mind representing yourself. Where does your mind stand? If your mind is set on the flesh, that means you are standing with Satan. If your mind is set on the spirit, that means you are standing with God. Therefore, the central point, the main thing, today is the attitude of the mind.

Now we realize why in Romans 12:2 the apostle said that we need to be transformed by the renewing of the mind. In Romans 8:2 there is the law of the Spirit of life. Then in Romans 8:6 there are two possibilities. We may stand either with the flesh or with the spirit. If we stand with the flesh, we are in death. If we stand with the spirit, we are in life. Romans 8:29 says that we have "to be conformed to the image of His Son." By the renewing of our mind we are transformed and conformed to the image of Christ. Also, by being transformed we will realize that the good, well-pleasing, and perfect will of God is the Body life revealed in Romans 12.

Romans 8 reveals that we have the law of the Spirit of life within us. If we stand with this law, we will be transformed and conformed to the image of Christ. Then Romans 12 shows that by our being transformed, we realize the good will of God, which is to have the Body life. Hence, the church life is a life of transformation, a life in which Christ as the Spirit is transforming us all the time.

THE TRANSFORMATION OF OUR INWARD PARTS

You may feel that several brothers are good brothers. But do not assume that they are without problems. Because they are not transformed, they can be very troublesome brothers. They are good, yet so natural. One of them may be naturally quick, and another one may be naturally meticulous. One is very fast, and the other is overly concerned with details. According to the fact that they have Christ within them, no doubt, they are members of the Body. But their natural man has no part in the Body.

Of course, the problem is not with the Christ within but with their being so natural without. When one who is naturally quick and one who is naturally meticulous come together to serve the Lord, they will have problems with each other. This does not mean that the Christ within this one is fighting with the Christ within the other one. It means that the quick one is fighting with the meticulous one. Both are members of Christ, but both are human. They are good, but they are humanly good, naturally good. This is the problem.

Hence, we need the transformation in our inward parts through the Spirit. At the time we were saved, the Lord Jesus as the Spirit of life came into us as the one law regulating our inward parts. One law in many parts means one law with many functions. When the Spirit as the one law permeates our mind, He becomes the law of the mind, regulating our thoughts and our way of thinking. When He permeates our emotion, He becomes the law of the emotion, regulating and ruling over what we like or dislike. When He permeates our will, He becomes the law of the will, regulating and governing our making of decisions. Thus, there is one law becoming three kinds of laws. But actually, they are not three laws but three functions of one law.

When the Spirit as the law regulates us in our inward parts, we are being transformed. How much we will be transformed depends on how much we are willing to be regulated by Him. If we are willing to be regulated by Him in our mind, our mind will be transformed. That means our mind will be permeated and saturated by Him and with Him. Our mind will be filled with Christ. Our thoughts and the way we think will be full of Christ.

If we allow Him to regulate our emotion, He will permeate our emotion. Then our desires, our preferences, will be filled with Christ. This means we are being transformed in our emotion. Whatever we like or desire will have the image, the expression, of Christ. Moreover, if we allow Him to govern, rule over, our will, our will will be possessed by Him and be full of Him. Then whatever we decide will have the flavor of Christ. This is the transformation of our inward parts by the wonderful Spirit. He is the law of life within us, living, moving, working, shining, illuminating, regulating, ruling, and governing within us.

LEARNING TO BE AN INWARD CHRISTIAN, TO BE TRANSFORMED FROM WITHIN, FOR THE PRACTICE OF THE CHURCH LIFE

Brothers and sisters, I look to the Lord that our eyes may

be opened to see that with us Christians it is not a matter of changing things outwardly. It is not that formerly we had hatred but now we try to cultivate love because we are taught that hatred is not good. It is not that formerly we had pride but now we pray to the Lord to give us humility, since we are taught that pride hurts, damages, and spoils things. Nor is it that formerly we easily lost our temper, but now we have learned to be patient because we found out from Proverbs that patience is desirable and profitable.

We may have some changes outwardly, but what about inwardly? The human way, the religious way, the way of Christianity, is to improve man in his outward conduct and behavior. The Lord's salvation, however, is to transform us from within. He wants to spread out from our very center, saturating and permeating all our inward parts with Himself. In this way we will be transformed from within. Then there will be no need for us to get rid of the troublesome, outward things. Because of the maturity and the growth of the inner life, all the troublesome, outward things will spontaneously be dropped. The life for the practice of the church life is a life of transformation by the Spirit.

When you are being transformed by this wonderful One, many times you experience the effectiveness of the all-inclusive death of Christ on the cross. Something within kills your desire, your motive, your intention. Sometimes when you are being transformed, you sense the release, the liberty, and the glorification. Something within makes you want to shout, "Hallelujah!" And sometimes when you are being transformed, you sense the government, the headship, and the lordship of Christ. You sense that the very Christ is on the throne, and He is the real King to you. Furthermore, you sense that you are reigning with Him, and you are His co-partner in the kingship. On the one hand, you are ruled and governed by Him. On the other hand, you are ruling with Him and sitting on the throne with Him. Many times you have the sense of the Lord's divinity, humanity, and human living within you. You have the deep inner feeling that what the Lord is, what the Lord has, and what the Lord has done are realized in you.

The church life is Christ Himself as the Spirit permeating, saturating, and transforming us. When we are fully transformed and are full of Christ, we will become the living, real, practical members of Christ. Then it will be easy for us to be joined, knit, and built up together with others. This is to be built up not with something natural as wood, grass, and stubble, but with something transformed as gold, silver, and precious stones (1 Cor. 3:12). The church is not formed by organization and discussion and by electing a chairman, a secretary, and a treasurer. That is a religious organization. The church is organic, something growing up in life.

In order to have the church life, we need to go to the cross and take care of Christ, who is the wonderful Spirit within us. We need to take care of our inner feeling, inner guidance, inner shining, and inner registration. If we would go to the cross and realize Christ within us, we will be clear. All problems are solved by the cross. This is why in 1 Corinthians 2:2 the apostle Paul told the believers that he did not determine to know anything among them except Jesus Christ and this One crucified. The church life is a transformed life, not a natural life. It is Christ Himself, not as an objective doctrine but as the subjective Spirit living within us.

Let us learn the lesson of being an inward Christian, not an outward Christian. Do not try to change yourself outwardly. That is false. You have to be transformed from within to become a living member of the Body; then you will realize the genuine church life. This is what we need today.

CHAPTER TEN

THE GIFTS FOR THE BUILDING UP
OF THE BODY

Psalm 68:18 says, "You have ascended on high; You have led captive those taken captive; / You have taken gifts among men, / Even the rebellious ones, / That Jehovah God may dwell among them." J. N. Darby rendered the second half of this verse as, "Thou hast received gifts in Man, and even for the rebellious, for the dwelling there of Jah Elohim." In Ephesians 4:8 Paul quotes this verse by saying, "Therefore the Scripture says, 'Having ascended to the height, He led captive those taken captive and gave gifts to men.'" *Those taken captive* refers to the redeemed saints, who were taken captive by Satan before being saved by Christ's death and resurrection. In His ascension Christ led them captive; that is, He rescued them from Satan's captivity and took them to Himself. In His ascension He made these rescued sinners gifts for the building up of His Body (vv. 11-12).

In order to understand Paul's thought in Ephesians 4:8, it will be helpful to know a little bit about the construction of this chapter. Verses 1 through 6 deal with the keeping of the oneness of the Spirit. The apostle first exhorted us to be diligent to keep the oneness of the Spirit. Then he pointed out seven things that form the base of our oneness: one Body, one Spirit, one hope, one Lord, one faith, one baptism, and one God. Based on these seven "ones" we have the oneness of the Spirit.

Then in verse 7 Paul said that "to each one of us grace was given according to the measure of the gift of Christ." We have received grace according to the measure of the gift of Christ. What does this mean? Just look at our own body. Each member of our physical body has a certain measure.

The measure of the nose is of one size, and the measure of the arm is of another. Because the arm is considerably bigger than the nose, it receives more supply of blood than the nose. The apostle Paul was a big member like an arm. Therefore, no doubt, a lot of grace was measured to him. We are small members like little fingers. Hence, the grace measured to us is not as great as what was measured to Paul.

The measure of the gift of Christ is the size of a member of His Body. Just as our blood supplies the members of our body according to their size, grace also is given to each member according to its size. In the Body of Christ there are different members and different gifts. Some are big members and some are small. Every member is a gift. The grace we receive is according to what we are as a member. One who is an apostle like Paul receives more grace than one who is a little member in the Body.

Now we go to verse 8, which says, "Therefore the Scripture says, 'Having ascended to the height, He led captive those taken captive and gave gifts to men.'" These "gifts" are not the abilities or capacities for various services, but the gifted persons mentioned in verse 11. Since verses 9 and 10 are parenthetical, verse 11 is a direct continuation of verse 8. Verse 11 says, "And He Himself gave some as apostles and some as prophets and some as evangelists and some as shepherds and teachers." It is clear that after His ascension Christ gave as gifts different gifted persons to the church. Verses 12 through 16 tell us that these gifted persons are for the perfecting of the saints unto the building up of the Body, that is, the church.

CHRIST ASCENDING TO THE HEAVENS
TO GIVE GIFTS TO MEN

When Christ received gifts in the heavens, He received them in man, as man. His standing, His qualification, for Him to receive the gifts was His being a man. We are men, and He represents us as a man. The gifts mentioned in Ephesians 4:8 are the gifted persons—apostles, prophets, evangelists, and shepherds and teachers. After conquering Satan and death and rescuing the sinners, the rebellious ones, from Satan and death through His death and resurrection, Christ in His ascension made the rescued sinners themselves such gifts by means of His resurrection life and gave them to His Body for its building up.

Consider the case of Peter. Before the day of Pentecost, he was not yet equipped to be an apostle. On the day of Pentecost, the ascended Christ as the wonderful Spirit came down from the heavens to qualify, to equip, him as an apostle. From that day on, Peter was an apostle as a gift given to the church by the Head. Also, consider the apostle Paul. Before the Lord's ascension, he was called Saul (Acts 13:9). As a young man, Saul helped the persecutors in their slaying of Stephen (7:58). Later, he devastated the church and perse-cuted the believers of Christ (8:3). After the Lord's ascension, however, the Lord came down to visit Saul and to enter into Saul. Thus, Saul was regenerated, transformed, equipped, and made an apostle as a gift given to the church.

After His ascension to the heavens, the Lord accomplished everything. As the One with divinity and humanity, He lived a human life, went through death, dealt with sin, overcame Satan, conquered death, released Himself as life, was glori-fied in His resurrection, ascended to the heavens, and was enthroned to receive the kingdom and authority. In Him is embodied all the fullness of the riches of the Godhead. When this One with so many things comes into us, He makes us gifts to the church.

Why does the Lord receive gifts for His Body in man, as man, on the standing of man, with the nature of man, and with the qualification of man? It is simply because we, the rebellious ones, are men. Our standing, our qualification, our nature, is that of a man. So the Lord must be the same as we are. If we give the full ground to Him, He can work out something in us to make us gifts to the church.

We should have an aspiration to be gifts to the Lord's Body. We should not be ambitious for any kind of position or title. We human beings want to be great, to be rich, to be famous, and to get some titles. Even among the so-called servants of God, many are seeking the worldly titles. They like to be advertised as "Dr. So-and-so" or "the world famous preacher." Some preachers would even receive an honorable degree. We should consider ourselves in this matter. Are you willing to be small, to be lowly, and to be poor? Are you willing to suffer opposition and persecution? Are you willing to be hidden, buried, and not to be famous? When the Lord was on this earth, in His human life He was willing to be lowly, poor, and buried. He was willing to suffer opposition and persecution. He never sought fame for Himself. If we desire to be famous in the religious world, in the Christian world, this means that we do not give ground to Christ in His human living. The all-inclusive Christ within us includes the element of His human living on this earth, which was lowly, poor, humble, restricted, and under persecution. Consider the apostles such as Peter and Paul. They experienced poverty, opposition, and persecution.

He who suffers the most will have Christ the most and will become the biggest part, the biggest member, of Christ. He who has more experiences of the cross will have more of Christ. How much of the cross has been applied to you? Is there ground within you for the death of Christ? If another brother quarrels with you and makes you unhappy, what should you do? If you fight back, this means there is no ground within you given to the death of Christ. But if you realize that you have been crucified with Christ and apply that death to yourself, this will cause you to have more of Christ and will make you a bigger part of Christ. You should say, "Lord, I am finished. I am on the cross. Now Lord, it is You who live in me."

Brothers and sisters, if you are willing to give more ground to Christ and the cross, you will have Christ with all His accomplishments. Christ's ascension and enthronement will be in you. You will be submitting to Christ as the King, and you will be a co-king, co-ruler, with Him. You will be on the throne with authority. Furthermore, you will realize and apprehend the transcendency, the power, the riches, and the fullness of Christ. All these things will be in you, and you will become a great part of Christ. Then you will become a real gift from the Head to the church.

Many think that if they are going to serve the Lord, they

need to go to a seminary or a Bible institute and study all the things about God. Then they can become a pastor, a minister, or a preacher to serve the Lord's children. This, however, is not the right way. You have to realize that Christ today is within you. Furthermore, everything that He has accomplished, obtained, and attained is also within you. You have to give Him the ground and let Him work Himself and everything that is of Him into you. Then you will be renewed, transformed, and re-made into something other than yourself. You will be made a part of Christ as a gift to be a great help to the saints. You will be able to perfect the saints for the building up of the Body. The real gifts for the building up of the Body of Christ are the persons who have been worked on by Christ in such a way that they are saturated and permeated with Christ so that they become the great parts of Christ.

These gifted persons should not do anything to replace the saints in the service of the Lord. Rather, they should perfect the saints to serve the Lord. Let me illustrate. Suppose I am a cooking expert. When I come to your home, there are two possibilities. One possibility is that I will get rid of you. I will tell you, "Brother, since you don't know how to cook, you had better stay away and let me cook for you." The other possibility is that I teach you how to cook and help you to cook. Then after a while you will be able to cook as I do because you have been perfected by me. The gifted persons should learn to perfect the saints in this way. They should not take their place in serving the Lord. They should not be their substitute. Rather, they should help them, teach them, and instruct them so that they may be perfected.

THE WAY TO PERFECT THE SAINTS

Now we need to see the way to perfect the saints. The gifted persons need to minister Christ to others. They have to help others realize Christ, know Christ, experience Christ, and grow in Christ. This is the intention, the ultimate goal, of the teaching of the apostles.

THE WINDS OF TEACHING

Ephesians 4:14 says, "That we may be no longer little

children tossed by waves and carried about by every wind of teaching in the sleight of men, in craftiness with a view to a system of error." Here I would ask you to mark or underline the word "teaching." This verse does not speak of the wind of heresy, nor the wind of mere doctrines, nor the wind of wrong teachings. It simply says "every wind of teaching."

Recently, I gave some messages in a conference, and there were three to five brothers there who would challenge me with some questions after each meeting. They came to me asking, "Brother Lee, what about predestination?" "What about absolute grace?" "What about the free will?" If I had spent the time to talk, discuss, and argue with them about all these matters, all the meetings there might have been spoiled. These kinds of teachings are like the wind blowing people away from Christ. Sometimes the wind may become a hurricane that can bring in a lot of damage. It causes people to forget about Christ and His expression, His Body. Instead, they begin to argue about different kinds of opinions and doctrinal matters. This is to be carried about by the wind of teaching.

In verse 14 the apostle mentioned the wind of teaching, and in the previous verse he mentioned the oneness of the faith. The oneness of the faith is something altogether contrary to the wind of teaching. Suppose five of us brothers come together. We have been regenerated and saved. We are in Christ and we are one. We have the oneness of the faith. We praise the Lord together, pray together, worship God together, and fellowship with one another. It is really good and wonderful. Then, one day, one of the brothers asks a question, "Brother Lee, how about the rapture?" Right away there is a danger, even a snare, before us. If we are not careful, we will open all the windows for the wind to blow in. Then we can no longer pray together because of our different views about the rapture. Eventually, we may even become divided and separated from one another.

If you have learned the lesson, it is better not to ask this kind of question. And if you are asked this kind of question, you have to learn to say, "Brother, anyhow, one day He will come to take us. Let us love Him and live by Him." This is the best answer. Do not allow yourself to be tempted to argue about doctrines. Keep yourself from being carried away by the wind of teaching. As long as you have the oneness of the faith, it is good enough. The faith consists of the seven "ones" in Ephesians 4: one Lord, one God, one Spirit, one Body, with one faith, one baptism, and one hope. As long as we have these seven "ones," it is sufficient.

Then verse 15 says, "But holding to truth in love, we may grow up into Him in all things, who is the Head, Christ." The truth is the reality, which is Christ Himself. We have to hold to Christ and grow up into Him in all things. Then, what is the outcome? Verse 16 says, "Out from whom all the Body, being joined together and being knit together through every joint of the rich supply and through the operation in measure of each one part, causes the growth of the Body unto the building up of itself in love." This means that out from the fountainhead, the source, the all-inclusive Head, we will receive something of Christ and minister something of Christ to one another. In this way there will be a great measure of Christ within us and among us. So we will have the growth of life and the transformation of life. Eventually, the Body will be built up by itself in love.

Brothers and sisters, this is the life for us to practice the church. I do ask you to pray about all these things that you may see something in these days.

2-26-95

CHAPTER ELEVEN

THE GROWTH AND THE BUILDING

Scripture Reading: 1 Pet. 2:2-5; 1 Cor. 3:7-13, 16-17; Eph. 2:21-22; 4:13-16

In this chapter we want to fellowship concerning the building up of the church by the growth in life.

THE GROWTH IN LIFE FOR THE BUILDING UP OF THE BODY OF CHRIST

First of all, we want to consider several passages in the Bible that link together the growth in life and the building of the church. First Peter 2:2-5 says that if we have tasted the Lord, not only believed in Him, we will long for the nourishing milk in His word and then we will grow (vv. 2-3). By this growing, we will be built up as a spiritual house (v. 5). Hence, these few verses show us mainly two things: one is the growth in life and the other is the building up of a spiritual house. The building up of the church as a spiritual house depends upon the growth in life. We are built up by growing in the life of Christ. Hence, growing is for building up, and building up depends on growing.

Now let us read 1 Corinthians 3:7-9: "So then neither is he who plants anything nor he who waters, but God who causes the growth. Now he who plants and he who waters are one, but each will receive his own reward according to his own labor. For we are God's fellow workers; you are God's cultivated land, God's building." Notice here that the apostle used two kinds of description for the church. First, he likened the church to God's cultivated land, God's farm, God's plantation, God's husbandry. Then, he likened the church to God's building. With the cultivated land, the farm, there is the need for growth. With the building, or the house, there is the need for building up. Verses 10 through 13 tell us what kind of materials should be used for the building.

Then verses 16 and 17 go on to say, "Do you not know that you are the temple of God, and that the Spirit of God dwells in you? If anyone destroys the temple of God, God will destroy him; for the temple of God is holy, and such are you." The temple of God in verse 16 refers to the believers collectively in a certain locality, whereas the temple of God in verse 17 refers to all the believers universally. All the believers are the unique temple of God in the universe, which has its expression in many localities on the earth. The temple is the building, and the building depends upon the growth of the cultivated land.

Furthermore, we can see the matter of growth and building in Ephesians 2:21-22. Verse 21 says that in Christ "all the building...is growing into a holy temple in the Lord." Not only are we being built up, but we are also growing into a temple. Then verse 22 says, "In whom you also are being built together into a dwelling place of God in spirit." Again, we see that the building up of the church as the dwelling place of God depends on the growth in life.

Then in Ephesians 4:13-16 we see again that the building depends on the growth. Verse 13 says, "Until we all arrive at the oneness of the faith and of the full knowledge of the Son of God, at a full-grown man, at the measure of the stature of the fullness of Christ." Verse 14 goes on to say that "we may be no longer little children...." We are no longer little children because we have grown up. Verse 15 says, "But holding to truth in love, we may grow up into Him in all things, who is the Head, Christ." We have to grow up into Christ, who is the Head of the Body. Then verse 16 tells us that out from the Head, Christ, "all the Body...causes the growth of the Body unto the building up of itself in love." In brief, this passage shows us that the building up of the Body, the church, depends on the growth of life in Christ.

THE NEED FOR A VISION OF GOD'S GOAL

The burden of this book is to show the Lord's children that in these last days the Lord is going to recover this one thing, that is, Christ being wrought into the believers in order to be mingled with them, and all the believers being transformed in nature, in essence, in element, and in their very human substance into the image of Christ. Then we will become the many parts of Christ to constitute the Body of Christ, the living expression of Christ. This is our burden, our vision, our revelation. This is also the mark or goal of our seeking.

The religious people tell us that we human beings need a religion. They are wrong. What we need is Christ. Christ is the center, and Christ is everything. Christ is the hope of glory within us (Col. 1:27) as the transforming life. He is transforming us day by day from an earthly person into a heavenly person. When we are completely transformed from within to without, from our spirit to our mind, emotion, and will, we will become living members of Christ. Then we will spontaneously grow together. Christ is in us, transforming us to make us grow into one. Then we will be the Body in reality. So the Body is built up by the growth in life.

Do you think we can come together to build up the church by discussion? Do you think some brothers can build up the church by agreeing on certain matters? Maybe this time we can agree with one another after a lengthy discussion, but I am afraid that after a while something will come out of us to contradict one another. Then we will fight with one another and have more discussions. If we do this, we are forming a religious body or organizing a Christian "church." This is not the building up of the Body of Christ.

The church as the Body of Christ is something growing up in Christ and into Christ. You have to grow, and I have to grow. The more we grow, the more we will be built up together. This building up is not by organization but by the growth in life.

God's goal, God's mark, is not merely to make us good persons. God's goal is to make us a part of Christ. For this we do not need so many doctrinal teachings. What we need is to grow up. We need to realize that Christ as the living One is the wonderful Spirit living within us. We need to contact Him.

Have you seen this vision concerning God's goal? I would suggest that after reading this chapter, you find a time to be with the Lord. Have a genuine prayer before Him and ask Him to show you His goal, His mark. You may pray, "Lord, reveal this matter to me and open my eyes that I may see a vision, that I may have a revelation concerning Your Body, concerning Your goal, Your mark." You should pray in this way at least once, and the more the better.

Many years ago, for a long time day by day I prayed about this matter. Every day I had a living prayer before the Lord: "Lord, open my eyes that I may see Your purpose, Your mark, Your goal. I have studied the Word for many years, but I don't know Your purpose, Your mark, Your goal, in the whole universe. Lord, reveal this to me. Open my eyes that I may see." I praise the Lord that He answered my prayer. At a certain time I was truly brought into the realization concerning the eternal purpose of God. Something so real was clearly revealed to me. I cannot deny that I did see something.

Following this, you need to have a definite and fresh consecration before the Lord. In Romans 12, before going into the truth of the Body, the apostle exhorted us to consecrate ourselves as a living sacrifice to God for His purpose and goal (v. 1). Maybe you have offered yourself already, but you need to offer yourself once again for the purpose of realizing God's eternal goal.

If you would do these two things—have a genuine prayer before the Lord and offer yourself again to Him—I have the full assurance that you will have a clear vision about yourself. You will see that your very self is good for nothing but death and burial. You will realize the cross of Christ. All the time you will have the sense that you have been put on the cross and terminated by the cross. You are good for nothing but to be crucified.

At the same time, you will also have the sense, the registration, the apprehension, the realization, that the all-inclusive Christ is so real to you and that He is living and working in you. Then you will be brought into the reality of Christ as life, light, the law of life, and the anointing. So day by day you will experience something living, working, acting, moving, enlightening, regulating, and anointing within you all the time. You will know how to go along with Christ, not an objective Christ in the heavens but a subjective Christ in your spirit and heart.

Furthermore, you will always sense that you are one with Him. While you pray, He prays in you. While you walk, He walks in you. While you go to certain places, He goes with you and in you. You will always sense His presence, not just beside you but within you. And you will realize how real and available He is.

Unconsciously and spontaneously you will gradually be transformed in many things—in your way of thinking, in your desire, in your emotion, in your intention, in your attitude, and in all of your inward parts. You will be wholly occupied and possessed by Christ and filled with Christ. Because you are so saturated and permeated with Christ, all things other than Christ will gradually be dropped by you. Day by day something will be dropped. Then you will grow up into Him. You will grow to such an extent that it will become easy for you to be joined together and knit together with all those who love the Lord. Eventually, you will have the reality of the Body of Christ, the reality of the church life.

Brothers and sisters, I believe that I have suggested the best way that can help us to see the vision of God's goal concerning the building up of the church. In brief, first, you have to realize that you have to die. If you are still living, there is no church life. You have to see that you need to be crucified and that you have been crucified (Rom. 6:6; Gal. 2:20). Second, you have to realize that Christ today is not only in heaven but also in you to be everything to you. Third, learn to go to Christ and contact Him by prayer. Do not pray for your own welfare. Instead, pray concerning Christ and the Body. Pray that you may see the living Christ within you. At the same time, offer yourself purposely and definitely for this matter. Tell the Lord, "Lord, I am here ready for Your purpose, for Yourself, for the experiencing of Yourself, and for the realization of Yourself." Fourth, learn to always maintain a good fellowship with the Lord who is in you. Go along with Him and take care of the inner anointing, the inner registration. These four points are good enough. If you practice them, many wonderful things will come out of you.

OUR NEED TO EXPERIENCE
THE LIVING CHRIST WHO DWELLS IN US

Now I want to mention three main categories of things which perplex today's Christians. First, there are the formalities of Christianity, including forms, rituals, regulations, etc. Next, there are a lot of teachings and doctrines. Last, there are the gifts. Brothers and sisters, allow me to tell you humbly but frankly that you do not need any kind of forms, rituals, regulations, rules, charters, constitutions, etc. What you need is the living Christ. Then, how about the teachings? I would not say that you do not need any kind of teaching. You need some teaching. But the teachings must be something for Christ and of Christ. They must help you to know Christ and experience Christ.

Now concerning the gifts, I would say that you and I do need some gifts. But we need to realize that gifts are merely gifts, not Christ Himself. Gifts are not for gifts but for Christ. All the gifts must be a help for us to know Christ, to know life, and to experience Christ as life. Do not be satisfied with the gifts. Gifts only open the door and pave the way for us to go to Christ.

Therefore, what you need today is the living Christ. When you are fully saturated, permeated, filled, occupied, and possessed by Christ, you will become a part of Christ and your very person will become a living gift. Wherever you go and wherever you are, you will be a great help to the church and to the children of God. Your person will be a real ministry of life to others. Then automatically the church life will come out. Today what we, the Lord's people, need is the living Christ constituted and wrought into us for us to be made parts of Christ. This is God's goal, God's mark, God's eternal purpose.

The most important lesson that we need to learn, however, is to experience Christ as the wonderful Spirit working, regulating, and moving within us. We need to take care of

this One. One time a brother came to me, saying, "Brother
Lee, I have something to talk with you about." But I knew
in my spirit that he came to quarrel with me. So I asked
him if at that moment he had the inner anointing to talk
with me. He replied, "To be honest with you, I don't have the
inner anointing. But I still want to talk with you." Many
times we have done the same thing. We know that we do not
have the anointing to do a certain thing, but we still want
to do it. This is a problem.

Many times even while you are going to preach the gospel,
you are disobedient to the inner anointing. And sometimes
while you are praying, you are disobedient to the inner
anointing. Within you the anointing tells you to pray for a
certain thing, yet you do not pray according to the anointing.
Rather, you want to pray in your way. The more you pray,
the more you sense you are disobeying the anointing. Again,
I say, this is our problem.

If we all simply take care of the inner anointing, there
will be no quarrel, argument, or hatred. Instead, there will
be harmony, oneness, love, unity, and the building up among
us. The building up of the church does not depend on anything
else but the growth in life by constantly taking care of the
inner anointing. Therefore, we need to learn to exercise our
spirit to take Christ as our life and to go along with the inner
anointing. In this way we maintain a good fellowship with
Him and are one with Him all the time.

Let us forget about so many things in our Christian
background and just be so simple before the Lord. We have
been crucified with Christ, and it is no longer we who live,
but it is Christ who lives in us (Gal. 2:20). This living Christ
as the Spirit is not far from us but right within us. He is so
available and practical. He is moving within us. I just
fellowship with Him and go along with Him.

Now you understand why in one of his hymns A. B.
Simpson said, "Oh! it is so sweet to die with Christ, / To the
world, and self, and sin; / Oh! it is so sweet to live with
Christ, / As He lives and reigns within" (*Hymns*, #482,
chorus). It is really so. It is so sweet to die with Christ, and
it is so sweet to live with Christ. Do not be complicated; just

be simplified. If you ask so many questions about this and that, I am afraid you are like a seminary student who has been complicated by a lot of study. In the Far East, I have met a great number of believers who are one hundred percent Gentiles without any Christian background. After they have been brought to the Lord, they are very simple. Many of them are highly educated people, yet they are wonderfully simple. It is so easy to help them to know Christ.

May the Lord have mercy on us that we may put aside everything from our old Christian background and just be so simple to go along with the living One who dwells in us. Then we will have the real Christian life and the real church life.

Chapter Twelve

THE WAY FOR THE PRACTICE
OF THE CHURCH LIFE

Scripture Reading: 1 Cor. 1:1-2; Rom. 16:16; 1 Cor. 14:33; Acts 8:1; 13:1; Rev. 1:11; 1 Cor. 1:12-13; 3:4-8, 21-23; 4:1, 6; Acts 28:30-31

With any kind of practice there is the need of two things: the life and the way. In the preceding chapters, we have seen the life for the practice of the church life. This is the life of Christ as the all-inclusive Spirit. We have this life within us. Now we need the way to match this life. In the next few chapters, we will cover the proper way for the practice of the church life.

We may liken the life to the wine and the way to the wineskin (Matt. 9:17). When you have the wine, you need the wineskin to contain the wine. We may also liken the life to the tea and the way to the teacup. If you have the tea, you need the teacup. We appreciate the tea and we are going to drink the tea, but we also need the teacup. This is why we are burdened concerning the way for the practice of the church life.

THE CHURCH OF GOD, THE CHURCHES OF CHRIST,
AND THE CHURCHES OF THE SAINTS

In order to help us understand this matter in an adequate way, I would ask you to read a number of passages from the Scripture. First, we want to read 1 Corinthians 1:1-2: "Paul, a called apostle of Christ Jesus through the will of God, and Sosthenes the brother, to the church of God which is in Corinth...." In this passage I would ask you to pay attention to this term "the church of God...in Corinth." The apostle used two phrases to qualify the church. First, it is the church

of God, and then it is the church in the place where the saints
are. The saints of Corinth were in the place of Corinth, so
their church was called the church in Corinth. Hence, we
have "the church of God...in Corinth." Then Romans 16:16b
says, "All the churches of Christ greet you." Furthermore,
1 Corinthians 14:33 says, "As in all the churches of the saints."

So in these three passages we have three terms: *the church
of God, the churches of Christ,* and *the churches of the
saints.* God, Christ, and the saints—these are the owners of
the church. The church is owned by God, by Christ, and by
the saints because the church is called the church of God, the
church of Christ, and the church of the saints. In the
Scripture you cannot find a passage that says the church is
the church of the apostles. You cannot find such a term
because the church or the churches are not something of the
apostles. The church is something of God, of Christ, and of
the saints. The apostles are not the owners of the church.
They are servants or ministers of the church. God and Christ
are the Owners of the churches, and the saints are also the
owners of the churches.

ONE CHURCH FOR ONE CITY,
ONE CITY WITH ONE CHURCH

In Acts 8:1 we have this expression—"the church which
was in Jerusalem." In the early days, the church in Jerusalem
had more than ten or twenty thousand members (Acts
21:20—note 20[1]). One day they had about three thousand
baptized (Acts 2:41), and then on another day they had about
five thousand (4:4). We are also told that the believers were
all the more being added to the Lord and that they multiplied
greatly (5:14; 6:1, 7). They had such a big membership and
they met in many homes, "breaking bread from house to
house" (2:46). Yet they were still called the church, the one
church (not the churches), in Jerusalem.

Now let us turn to Acts 13:1. This verse says, "Now there
were in Antioch, in the local church, prophets and teachers...."
Here it does not say "in Antioch, in the local churches," but
"in Antioch, in the local church." This indicates that in one
locality, in one place, in one city, there is only one local church.

Now let us read Revelation 1:11: "Saying, What you see write in a scroll and send it to the seven churches: to Ephesus and to Smyrna and to Pergamos and to Thyatira and to Sardis and to Philadelphia and to Laodicea." Verse 20 says, "The mystery of the seven stars which you saw upon My right hand and the seven golden lampstands: The seven stars are the messengers of the seven churches, and the seven lampstands are the seven churches." In these two verses we can see two things. The first thing is that there were seven churches in seven cities, indicating one church for one city, one city with only one church. The other thing is that the seven churches were seven lampstands. This indicates that the lampstand signifies the church. Regardless of how weak the churches are, they are still the lampstands. Even though John did have a strong and rich ministry, his ministry was not the lampstand. The lampstand is the church, not the ministry.

We have seen that God's eternal goal is to work Christ Himself into us that we may be the real parts of Christ as the living members of the Body of Christ, which is the church as the living expression of Christ. Now we have to see the proper way, the right way, the best way, for us to come together to practice this wonderful church life. We are not talking about the way to organize or to form something. We are talking here about the proper way for us to practice a living expression of Christ.

We all know that in the whole universe the church is one. There is one Christ, one Head, and one church, one Body. You cannot have one Christ and more than one church. You cannot have one Head with more than one Body. In the universe there is only one Christ, and this one Christ has only one Body. However, although the church is one in the universe, it is expressed on this earth in many places. This one church has many expressions. Because the church in the universe is one, the expression of the church in any place must also be one.

Let us illustrate in this way: Today if you go to Tokyo, which is a big city with millions of people, you cannot find two American embassies there. You can find only one

American embassy in Tokyo. Regardless of how big the city is, there can be only one American embassy. If there were two, that would mean that America is divided. When I go to Tokyo, there is no need for me to ask which American embassy I should go to. There is only one embassy in Tokyo representing America. The United States embassy in Tokyo is the very expression of the United States in that city. The United States is one, not two. So in any place, any embassy representing the United States must be one.

In the same principle, the church in the whole universe is one. So in any place, in any locality, if there is some expression of the church, that expression must be one. If we want to be in the proper way to practice the church, we must first remember that the church in the whole universe is one. So if we are going to express the church in any place, we must be one. In any locality there must be only one local church as a living expression of the Body of Christ. If there is more than one, that means division has taken place. This is exactly what has happened today. If you go to Tokyo, there is no need for you to inquire about what American embassy you should attend. But today when people go to a city, they ask about what church they should attend. There are many different kinds of churches today. This means divisions have occurred. Any denomination is a division. There should not be many different churches in one locality, that is, many different expressions of the Body of Christ in one city. In one city, there should be only one expression of the one Body of Christ.

THE FACTORS OF DIVISION

Divisions come into existence due to two factors. One factor is related to the Lord's servants. There is no doubt that the ministers, the servants, of the Lord work for the Lord by trying their best to help people through preaching and teaching. But eventually nearly all the servants of the Lord keep the results of their work in their hands. A servant of the Lord may be called by God and sent by the Lord with a real ministry and a real commission. Then he goes out to work for the Lord. He works hard and effectively to help people, and he eventually gains some real results. But the problem or the danger here is that this very servant of the Lord may keep the results of his work in his own hands to form something as a support to his work. If this happens, a division is created.

Let us illustrate in this way: Here is the apostle Paul, who is sent by the Lord with a real commission. He comes to Los Angeles and works very hard with much effectiveness. As a result, a great number of people are saved through him. So his work issues in a great result, and he keeps the result of his work in his hands for his ministry. Then after three years, Apollos comes. He is also sent by the Lord with a real commission. He works hard and effectively, and a great number of people are saved through him. Like Paul, he keeps his work in his hands and forms something in Los Angeles other than what Paul has formed. So now in Los Angeles there is something of the apostle Paul and there is something else of the Lord's servant Apollos. After another two years, Peter comes and he does the same thing as Paul and Apollos. So now in Los Angeles there are three groups of Christians. You should not call them churches. The best you can say is that they are three groups. No matter what you call them, whether denominations, missions, sects, congregations, assemblies, or "churches," they are divisions, and even if you call them nothing, they are still divisions.

Here the servants of the Lord have to learn the lesson from history. None of us should keep the work in our hands. We have to work for the Lord, for His church, and for the saints. The result, the issue, of the work must go to the saints. Nothing should be kept in the hands of any of the Lord's servants. Paul did go to Corinth and worked there effectively. Although many were saved through him, he did not set up his own group. He worked for the local church which was in Corinth. Apollos and Peter also did the same thing. There were not three "churches" in Corinth, one of Paul, another of Apollos, and still another of Peter. There was only one church in Corinth.

However, although Paul, Apollos, and Peter did not do this kind of divisive work, the pitiful Corinthian believers did something to separate themselves from one another (1 Cor. 1:12-13). Some would say, "I appreciate Paul. Paul is wonderful. I am of Paul." Others would say, "I appreciate Apollos. He is an eloquent man and is powerful in the Scriptures. I am of Apollos." And still others would say, "Peter is the greatest one. I am of Peter." Eventually, some would say, "You are all wrong. We do not belong to anyone. We belong to Christ alone, so I am of Christ." So there were four groups in Corinth, and they were condemned by the apostle for being carnal, fleshly (3:3-4). Look at today's Christianity, and you will see that the same situation exists there.

We must realize that the local churches do not belong to the apostles or the workers. As the churches of God (1:2), the local churches belong to God; as the churches of Christ (Rom. 16:16b), they belong to Christ; and as the churches of the saints (1 Cor. 14:33b), they belong to the saints. The churches must not belong to any of the workers. The churches are neither for the workers, the ministers, nor for the work, the ministry. Rather, the workers or ministers and their works or ministries must be for the churches. If I come here to carry out a work, and keep the results of my work in my hands, this is absolutely wrong. After much laboring, the apostle Paul had nothing in his hands. Everything was left in the hands of the local church.

You have to realize that as long as you keep the results of your work in your hands, you have a sect, a division, in your hands. You have to keep your hands off the results of your work and leave the results to the local saints. Let us follow the footsteps of the apostle Paul. Many churches were established through him, yet in the end he kept nothing in his hands. So Paul did not create any division.

Now we come to the second factor of divisions, which is related to having specialties. The divisions came into being because of the saints' having something special. According to church history, it is clear that soon after the time of the early apostles, the church deviated from the right track. It degraded and became a strict organization with the formation of the Roman Catholic Church. Then from the time of the Reformation, the state churches came into existence. These state churches are also organized churches. After the state churches, many saints saw particular spiritual things such as baptism by immersion, the presbyterial system, and holiness, sanctification, by faith. Those who saw something about baptism formed something to represent and maintain baptism. They made a mistake by making baptism by immersion something special, and they stood for this specialty. Then there were the Presbyterians, the Methodists, and so many other denominational churches. Thus, many divisions were created, and every division was for something special.

I was told that in a certain place there were two groups of believers. They were the same in nearly everything, but in one thing they were different. While one group insisted on not having a piano or organ, the other group insisted on having some kind of instrument for the music. Because of this, the original group was split into two—one group without any piano or organ and another group with a musical instrument.

I was brought up in Christianity and had learned to behave in the meetings in a quiet and nice way. One day in 1932, I attended a meeting which was somewhat under the influence of the Pentecostal movement. Brother Watchman Nee was invited to speak there. When I went into the meeting, some were laughing, clapping, and shouting "Hallelujah!" in a corner, some knelt down and were crying and weeping, some were dancing, and some were even rolling on the floor. I said to myself, "My goodness, what is this?" Then after a while, they all quieted down to listen to the message given by Brother Nee. After the meeting was over, while Brother Nee and I were walking back to the place where we stayed, I said to him, "Brother Nee, I cannot go along with that kind of meeting." He replied, "You cannot find any kind of regulation or any kind of form from the Scriptures concerning how we Christians should meet." That stopped my speaking. I must make it clear, however, that this does not mean that Brother Nee agreed with that kind of dancing, laughing, shouting, weeping, and rolling on the floor.

My point is that we all have to learn not to make ourselves special in anything. We do not represent anything but Christ.

Christ is the center, Christ is the circumference, and Christ is everything. Whenever we come together as the church, we do not and should not represent anything but the all-inclusive Christ. We are not for baptism, for speaking in tongues, for the breaking of bread, or for the order of the meetings. We are for Christ alone. This is easy to say but not easy to practice. One time a brother from a local church that uses grape juice for the Lord's table went to another locality where the saints use wine for the Lord's table. When he noticed the difference, he first hesitated and then he spoke a lot to express his disagreement. Brothers and sisters, we must maintain the proper attitude not to make anything special in the practice of the church. If you make something special, that means you become sectarian in that particular matter.

You may be in your locality going on in the way that you believe is decent, good, and in order. But if you go to some other places where they have some other ways to conduct their meetings and to arrange the seats, will you be able to refrain from saying anything and just go along with them? This is the biggest problem.

In conclusion, first, we have to realize that the church is one in the universe, so the expression of the church in any place must be one. As Christians coming together to express Christ in any locality, we should be one with one another. We should not keep ourselves separate from other Christians in the same locality. Second, all the workers must keep their hands off the work. They should leave the results of their work to the saints in the local church. Third, all the local churches must be very common, general, without anything special. If you keep anything special, you will be sectarian.

I believe in unity, but I do not believe in uniformity. Perhaps the saints in the church in Los Angeles meet in one way, and the saints in other localities meet in other ways. Do not try to make every place the same in everything. One local church may practice in one way, and another may practice in another way, yet they are still one. They are in the oneness, the unity. All these things seem complicated, but actually it is quite simple. In the early days, the Christians were very simple. They had no forms, no organization, no division, no regulations, etc. But they had the living Spirit within them. Wherever they went, they just gathered together to worship the Lord according to the leading of the Holy Spirit within them.

Today we should also make everything simple. Wherever we go and wherever we are, we have to be one with the other saints. In any place you should not separate yourself from other saints. As long as they are not divisive, you have to join them and be one with them. We may say that we are free, that we are not denominational, and that we are not sectarian, yet we are separated and would not come together as the one expression of the Body of Christ in this one city. This shows that we are wrong and is a real test to us, proving that we still have something which is not of the Lord. If we are really for the Lord and are absolutely of the Lord, we will come together in our locality as the one expression of the one Body of Christ. There is no reason and no right for anyone to keep his group separated from others. This is the test.

THE RELATIONSHIP AMONG THE CO-WORKERS

Now I want to add a little word concerning the relationship among the co-workers. In the Scriptures, in Acts and in the Epistles, you can see many people working for the Lord. But they were not organized together. There was no organization for the churches or for the co-workers, the apostles. Peter and some brothers worked in Jerusalem, in Judea, and Paul and others worked in the different places of the Gentile world. There was no organization of the co-workers, and there was no central control over them. They were all sent by the Lord and all worked for the local saints, for the local churches. None was organized with others and none would keep any work in his hands. So there was no problem. As long as we have organization, the problems will come.

Peter worked for the Lord, and Paul also worked for the Lord, but they were not organized together. Sometimes Paul went to Jerusalem to help the church there, and sometimes Peter came to other places where Paul worked to help the churches there. Peter and Paul, however, never formed an organization. Of course, we realize that Peter had a group of co-workers with him, and Paul had another group of co-workers with him. But their grouping was not an organization. They just went together to serve the Lord. There was neither financial control nor central control. Paul received the supply from the Lord for his own living, and his co-workers received the supply from the Lord for their own living. They just took care of one another in love. Since there was no organization among them, everything was so clear, free, and simple.

As long as we do not have any kind of organization, everything will remain simple and without trouble. Suppose I go to a certain locality to work. Eventually, I leave the results of my work in the hands of the local saints there. Then another brother goes there and works in the same way, and a third brother goes there and works in the same way. The church in that locality is not in the hands of any one of us.

Furthermore, we three even do not have any kind of organization. We are just working together for the Lord. By the Lord's guidance at the present time, we have to stay here to work together and go on together, but this is not an organization. I do not give either of them a salary, nor do they give me a salary. If you feel led by the Lord to work with me, let us go on together. If I feel guided by the Lord to work with you, let us go along together. If we do not have any guidance from the Lord to work together, we just go on with the Lord. It is so simple.

All the saints also come together on their own within their own jurisdiction to go on with the Lord. Maybe they feel they have to invite me to help them. Then they just do it. When they invite me and I feel guided by the Lord, I just go to them. Maybe they feel to invite another brother. Then they just do it, and this brother can go if he feels led of the Lord. So we see there is nothing organized and nothing is kept in the hands of the co-workers. All the results of the work are in the hands of the local saints meeting together as the local expression of the Lord's Body. This is according to the New Testament teaching and pattern.

Finally, I would speak a little word concerning the ministry meetings. The ministry meetings are meetings of the ministry to help the saints and the local churches. These meetings are for the local churches, but they are not local church meetings and are not in the hands of the local churches.

According to the pattern set up in the book of Acts, there are three ways for the servants of the Lord to work and minister to the saints. One is that, as a servant of the Lord, you can go to any locality to help the church there. You can attend the church meetings and take the opportunity to minister to the saints.

Another way is that you can be in a place where there is a local church, yet at the same time you can rent a place for your ministry. Paul did this when he was in Rome. In Acts 28 we are told that while Paul was in Rome, for two years he rented a house for himself to work and "welcomed all those who came to him, proclaiming the kingdom of God and teaching the things concerning the Lord Jesus Christ" (vv. 30-31). Paul did not form another group by his ministry. The fruit of his ministry was for the church in Rome. Remember that you should not form anything of your own to keep the results of your ministry. All the results of your ministry must go to the local church.

The third way is that if you stay in a locality for a long time, spontaneously you become a member of the local church there and serve the Lord as a local member. Peter was an example of this. He stayed in Jerusalem for a long time, so he automatically served the Lord in the church in Jerusalem as a local member.

I hope this simple word may make the situation and the way clear to us.

CHAPTER THIRTEEN

THE ATTITUDE AND RELATIONSHIP OF THE WORKERS

In the previous chapter, we mentioned something concerning the attitude and relationship of the workers. In this chapter we will continue to cover this matter in a more thorough way.

Most of the divisions among Christians were brought in by the workers. The history of the church shows that the more workers were raised up by the Lord, the more divisions were created. No doubt, John Wesley was a person greatly gifted by the Lord, but I regret to say that even he brought in a division, the so-called Methodist church. We have to learn the lesson from history.

All the workers are in a dangerous position of bringing in a sect. Many times I have said to myself that it is dangerous and tempting for us, the workers, to bring in some sects and cause some divisions. Today a number of us brothers are learning to serve the Lord. We hope that the Lord would grant us not only a gift but also a ministry and that we could be used by the Lord. But we have to be very careful. Otherwise, perhaps after fifteen years there will be as many sects as the number of full-time co-workers we have here today. If we have seven or eight workers today, we could have seven or eight sects fifteen years from now. From history we can see that nearly all the gifted persons were sect creators. There was hardly any exception.

We brothers who are workers of the Lord need to be clear that if we are not careful we will be the sect creators. The more we work, the more we do, and the more we labor, the more we are in danger of creating a sect. Furthermore, the more we are used by the Lord, the greater is the danger of our creating a sect.

We saw in the past, again and again, that on the one hand, the gifted persons rendered much help to the church, yet on the other hand, the gifted persons perplexed and, to some extent, damaged the church. On the one hand, the saints received great benefit through the gifted persons, but on the other hand, the saints were perplexed and complicated by the gifted persons.

Because of this, you have to learn how to receive the ministry, the help, from the gifted persons and how to discern the help from the complication. Do not follow the ministry or the workers blindly. Do not say, "I receive a great help from this person. Everything is all right. I just follow him." You should not do this. You should not follow anyone blindly or reject anyone blindly. You need to have the discernment. Anything of one's ministry that is profitable and helpful, you should receive; whatever is complicating and perplexing, you should reject.

OUR WORK BEING TO MINISTER CHRIST AND TO BUILD UP THE CHURCH

Dear brothers, as the workers, as the servants of the Lord, in the New Testament age, first, you have to see that your work, your ministry, is to preach or minister Christ and to build up the church. These two items must be the governing rules. Wherever you go and whatever you do, you must be governed, ruled, by these two items.

You should not go to any place to preach immersion or predestination. What you should preach and minister is Christ Himself. God has no intention to tell people about immersion or predestination. God also has no intention to tell people about prophecy. If prophecy is a help for people to know Christ, that is all right. But if that becomes a factor to draw people away from Christ, you have to give it up. The ministry of the Lord's servants in this present age is nothing else than to preach and minister Christ to others and to build up the church. You should not preach anything but Christ, and you should not work for the building up of your work, your ministry, but for the building up of the church. If any servant of the Lord breaks these two rules, you can be assured that he is sectarian. This is something very basic, about which we all need to be clear.

We are sent by the Lord to preach Christ either as the Savior to the sinners or as the all-inclusive Christ to the saints. We have to preach, to minister, Him to people with the building up of the church in view. If the view of your work is to enlarge and build up your ministry, that is absolutely wrong. You must preach Christ with only one intention, one purpose, and that is to build up the saints as a local church to express Christ in a corporate way.

NOT KEEPING THE RESULTS
OF OUR WORK IN OUR HANDS

Another thing which we, the workers, have to be careful about and which was mentioned already in the preceding chapter is that we should not keep any of the results of our work in our hands. This is the pattern set up by the apostle Paul. In the first journey of his ministry, wherever Paul went, he preached the gospel, and a number of believers were raised up. Then Paul helped them to be the local church in their respective place. All the results of his ministry went to the local churches. He kept nothing for himself.

However, if you look into history, there are many real stories indicating that a great many of the Lord's workers did not follow Paul's example. Let me give you a small illustration. In the years between 1925 and 1927, due to a great change in the political circle in China, there was an influence demanding all the Western missionaries to turn over everything of their work to the local Chinese Christians. The Presbyterian missionaries, however, insisted on keeping everything in their hands. Consequently, some of the local saints left the Presbyterian church.

We have to realize that we are not sent out to build up our ministry. We are sent out to build up, to perfect, the saints for the building up of the Body of Christ. However, it is easy for us to keep the results of our work in our hands with the good excuse, even the best excuse, that we are protecting the saints. We may say, "Look, these people are so young; they are even babies. They don't know anything. I have to take care of them. I am the parent, so I have to protect them as my children."

One time I was invited to a certain place. I was placed in a specially prepared building and treated as the most honorable guest. During my stay, various people came to see me and told me their feelings. Nearly all of them were seeking ones. The inner registration I had concerning their situation can be illustrated by the following description. These friends were like a big family. They had a very capable father, and this father loved all his children very much. Some children were nearly forty years of age. They simply wanted to get married and have their own family. But the father still treated them as babes. The father explained to me, saying, "They are still young." The children, on the other hand, said to me, "Brother Lee, we have been here for many years. We have nothing to do." Brothers, here you see the problem.

Other workers might give some mean excuses for keeping the work in their hands. Some might say, "I have been working and laboring here for many years. If I don't keep the result of the work in my hands, I have no security." This kind of excuse is mean. If you want security, I would advise you to go to the world to get something as security. Do not come to work for the Lord to get some security. There is no security in the Lord's work. Anyone who comes to the Lord's work must be ready to sacrifice everything, even his life. If you do not want to be this kind of person, I advise you not to touch the Lord's work. It is better for you to get a job in the world.

If I try to keep anything of my work here in Los Angeles in my hands, this becomes a sect. Regardless of how I declare and proclaim it, it is a sect. But if all the results of my work go to the church here, then the local church here has its own jurisdiction and its own liberty. The church here has a free hand to go on with the Lord. Suppose the saints in the church here feel the need to invite a worker from Texas. They have the full liberty to invite him. If they feel the need to invite another one from Europe, another one from Africa, and another one from South America, they have the full liberty to do so. This is the proper way for us to practice.

In 1934 the Lord was moving among the Chinese young believers. They saw something about the church, and that had an influence on the work of the China Inland Mission. The CIM missionaries gathered in Shanghai to have a conference to discuss how to handle the situation. They knew that the situation was due mostly to the work among us, so some of them had some contact with Brother Watchman Nee. Brother Nee talked with them according to the truth. He told them, "You brothers have sacrificed your country, your family, and a lot of other things to come to China to work for the Lord. I believe your intention is to build up the Body of Christ." They replied, "Right, Brother Nee. We are here to build up the Lord's Body." Then Brother Nee said, "Wonderful! We are doing the same thing. Then let us work together." But eventually, it became clear that the CIM missionaries were not willing to give up the so-called CIM Church.

Then Brother Nee told them, "If your coming and staying here is to build up your CIM Church, this is a big difficulty. If you would be willing to keep your hands off your work and let the believers be the local churches, everything would be all right." Then the missionaries replied, "We are not a denomination. We are just a mission—the China Inland Mission." Brother Nee said, "It is good that you are just a mission, but the mission has to keep its hands off the churches. As a mission, you should not form a mission church." Eventually, they were not able to get through in this matter. Many missions went to China, but unfortunately, instead of building up local churches in China, the missions built up their respective mission churches. This became a problem to the Chinese saints.

Our work is to build up local churches for the building up of the Body of Christ. We should not be afraid that if we keep our hands off the local churches, they will be carried away. Do not be afraid that a local church will be carried away. If it can be carried away, let it be carried away. Do not take the excuse that you are going to be the custodian to protect the little children. The Lord is the Custodian; you are not the custodian. You are just a servant of the Lord serving His children.

NOT IMPOSING ANYTHING
ON THE SAINTS AND THE CHURCHES

Also, as a worker, as a servant of the Lord, wherever you go you should not impose anything on the saints and on the local churches. You should not push anything or touch anything that may become a factor of creating division.

Suppose you are a worker of the Lord and are also very much for speaking in tongues. One day you come to Los Angeles and find out that the church here does not pay attention to speaking in tongues and may even take the attitude of being against it. Perhaps in the first two weeks you do not say anything about it, but probably in the third week the "fox tail" will come out. After another week, maybe you will stand up to impose something, saying, "Why don't you speak in tongues? What's wrong with speaking in tongues?" You may be able to convince a certain number to go along with you and get the same experience as you have had. Then a division is created.

What is the right attitude? Should you demand others to speak in tongues since you feel it is something right? None of us should give up anything that is genuine and right. But when you realize that the saints here do not feel happy about this matter, you have to be careful. If they ask you, "Do you speak in tongues?" you should answer, "Yes, but, brothers, I just minister Christ to others. Speaking in tongues is not my ministry. Of course, if any of you feel the need to speak in tongues, you just do it. But if you don't feel so, I'm really happy with you. As long as you love the Lord Jesus and you live by Him and glorify Him, I am absolutely for it." We should take such a liberal attitude in truth and in faithfulness. Some brothers would openly deny that they speak in tongues, but secretly try to push people into speaking in tongues. We should never be such two-faced persons.

Do you believe that only those who speak in tongues love the Lord? I do not believe so. In church history, many people who were spiritual and loved the Lord never touched the matter of speaking in tongues. Furthermore, in my Christian life I have seen many spiritual people who did not know anything about speaking in tongues yet who were full of life, power, and authority. In China I made a point to some who spoke in tongues by saying, "Brothers, look at this district. The people here never talk about speaking in tongues, but a great number of sinners have been saved through them. They love the Lord so much, and their preaching is prevailing. It is an undeniable fact. But look at the other district. The people there speak in tongues a lot, but where is the power?"

By this we see that there is no need for you to impose on others the matter of speaking in tongues. On the other hand, there is also no need for those who do not speak in tongues to oppose those who do. As long as people love the Lord Jesus, it is good enough. Let them be free.

If we take the right attitude, eventually the saints will realize that there is no need either to oppose speaking in tongues or to impose it on others. We just leave this matter in the hands of the Lord; we take a liberal attitude. If the Lord gives us this kind of gift, we just receive it from Him. But we would neither impose it nor oppose it. What difference does it make whether or not one speaks in tongues? All we care for is that people preach Christ as the living Savior and that they love Him, live by Him, exalt Him, express Him, and worship Him. This is the right attitude.

The same principle applies to immersion. I believe that baptism by immersion is the right thing, and I am one hundred percent for it. But if I come to this city and realize that the saints here practice sprinkling, I should not be surprised. I should just be happy, for a good number are saved and they love the Lord, seek the Lord, and live by the Lord. This is good enough. Whether they are baptized by immersion or by sprinkling does not mean much. Although I know what is right, I would not impress people with what I know. I would neither impose this nor oppose that. This is the right attitude. If someone comes to ask me with a sincere and proper spirit about this matter, I may fellowship with him, saying, "Brother, I feel that baptism by immersion is the right way, but I don't like to impose it. If you brothers feel that it is right to baptize people by sprinkling, just go ahead and do it. If you feel, however, that it is more right to have immersion, that is fine. Just do it."

We need to take such a liberal attitude toward all these things. Wherever we go, we have to be careful not to make anything a factor to create divisions, troubles, and problems among the saints. Always try your best to preach Christ, to minister Christ, to solve the problems instead of creating problems. Never have the intention to convince people to stand with you. If you, as a servant sent out by the Lord, have the intention to convince others to stand with you, that is very shameful. It is better that you go to the political circle to be a politician to win people for yourself.

Brothers, we are sent out by the Lord just to minister Christ to others and help others to know Him. We should be willing to be rejected. It is wrong to try to win people over to you. Wherever you go, never say anything different from the current situation there to create any division. For instance, concerning the Lord's table, you may be absolutely in favor of using one cup for the whole congregation. Suppose you go to a church where many small cups are used. Do not be surprised by it, do not talk about it, and do not even consider it. Just go along with it and take the small cup. Do not raise the question of whether one cup is right or many cups are right. We are not sent by the Lord to minister cups to people. Some people are legal in insisting on using one cup. In the end, they become spiritually dead. The Lord does not honor that. I do not mean, however, that everything is right. We know what is right and what is wrong, but there is no need to pay attention to these trivial things.

In Romans 14 the apostle Paul wrote concerning eating (vv. 2-3) and the keeping of days (vv. 5-6). He was very clear about what was right and what was wrong, but his attitude was not to impose anything upon others, not to push anything, and not to insist on anything. He took a very liberal attitude. As long as people receive Christ as their Savior, love the Lord, live to the Lord, and glorify the Lord as the all-inclusive One, that is good enough. If they keep the days, they keep them to the Lord; if they do not keep the days, they do not keep them to the Lord. As long as they do it to the Lord, it is good enough. This is the attitude we have to take. Then we will not bring damage to the saints and the churches, but we will be a help to them.

NOT HAVING ANYTHING ORGANIZED AMONG THE WORKERS

Furthermore, we should never have anything organized among the workers. Just as with the church nothing should be organized, so also with the workers nothing should be organized. You are just a servant of the Lord, and the others are also servants of the Lord. If you are asked to work with certain co-workers, you just come together by the Lord's guidance and go on to work together. Maybe this year we will work together, and the next year you will feel led by the Lord to go to another place. Whether we work together or we work separately, there is no problem. Whether we are here or we are there, we do not work for ourselves. Our intention is just to help people to know Christ and to be built up and strengthened as a local expression of His Body. If this is the case, there will be no trouble among us. But if we have something organized, a lot of problems will arise.

Furthermore, do not try to unify the work. Do not say, "We are in America, so we should be unified. Let us have a conference to unify the situation." This is wrong. We strongly insist on having the unity, but we are altogether against unification and uniformity. I have the full assurance that in the early days the churches in Judea were quite different from the churches in the Gentile world. The apostles did not try to unify the churches or make them uniform.

BEING LIBERAL

The church in Los Angeles may use one cup for the Lord's table, and the church in San Francisco may use many cups. That is all right. Let them be different. The brothers in one locality may practice immersion, and the brothers in another locality may practice sprinkling. Be liberal. Do not try to unify their action; do not try to make them uniform. What good is it for all of us to be unified or uniform? As long as our intention is to build up the Body of Christ, it is good enough.

Perhaps some will accuse me of being too liberal. Actually, I know which practice is better and which practice is inferior, but what I mean is that there is not much difference in reality, in spirituality, between this and that. There is no need to insist that everyone do the same thing.

All the local brothers and sisters have to learn the same lesson of being liberal. Whatever is good for helping people know Christ, we are for it. Whatever is good for the preaching of the gospel to get sinners saved, we have to be for it. However, whatever is divisive, factious, we must keep our hands off.

Do not say, "I am of Paul" or "I am of Apollos" or "I am of Peter." Do not regard someone as higher than others. If their ministry is a help to you, take it. You have to realize that you are not for any ministry, but you are for the church, for the expression of the Body of Christ. Do not say that you are for this brother or that brother. This is something fleshly (1 Cor. 3:4). We recognize that all the servants of the Lord are sent by the Lord and are given as gifts to His Body and that they have different ministries. We take all the good matters of these ministries. But if there is anything factious, divisive, we have to be careful.

None of us is here for the ministry. We are all here for the Body, the church. The workers should take the attitude that their work is not for their own ministry, and all the local saints should learn the lesson not to stand for anything other than the church. Simply stand for the local expression of the church because the local church, not the ministry, is the lampstand for Christ.

By the Lord's mercy, I am a brother with a ministry here. If the saints here are standing for my ministry instead of the local expression, I have to tell you that you are wrong. You should not stand for any ministry, even my ministry. What you have to stand for is the church, the local church. Any minister with any ministry or any worker with any work who comes here must be for the local church. If it is not for the local church, you have to say, "No, you are going to build up something other than the lampstand, something other than the local expression of the Body. We would not go along with this."

We know God's eternal purpose in this age is to build up the churches in different localities as the local expressions of Christ for the building up of the Body of Christ. We are absolutely for this. If we would all learn to take such an attitude, that would be a great help to the practice of the church life. What the Lord is going to build up is the local church, not the ministry, as the expression of Christ. The ministry is just a means, an instrument, for the Lord to build up the local church for the building up of the Body of Christ.

CHAPTER FOURTEEN

THE GROUND OF ONENESS

Scripture Reading: Deut. 12:5-8, 11-15, 17-18, 20-22, 26-27; 14:22-23; 15:19-20; 16:16-17

In this chapter we will go on to see something in more detail concerning the way for the practice of the church life.

Deuteronomy is a book which shows the proper way for the children of Israel as God's people, after their entrance into the land of Canaan, to have a life, a walk, or a living according to God's mind which would be well pleasing to God Himself. The holy living mentioned in the book of Deuteronomy is a living of worship, or service, to God. Our life must be a life that is absolutely dedicated to the worship, the service, of God.

THE GOOD LAND AS A TYPE
OF THE ALL-INCLUSIVE CHRIST

The things which the people of Israel experienced in the Old Testament are pictures, types, figures, and shadows, pointing us to the reality of the things in the New Testament time (1 Cor. 10:6, 11). The land of Canaan into which the children of Israel entered is a type of the all-inclusive Christ (Col. 1:12). God brought the children of Israel out of Egypt and transferred them into the land of Canaan to worship and serve Him. This typifies that God has delivered us out of the world, out of the authority of the darkness of Satan, and transferred us into Christ (v. 13). Now we are walking, living, working, and worshipping and serving God in Christ (2:6).

When the children of Israel were in Egypt, they had the lamb of the Passover, which is a type of Christ as the initiation of our experience of Him (1 Cor. 5:7). Our experience of Christ begins with the experience of Him as the redeeming Lamb.

Then after the children of Israel came out of Egypt, while they were wandering and traveling in the wilderness, they had the daily manna and the rock out of which flowed the living water (1 Cor. 10:3-4). These are further types of Christ. After we experience Christ as the redeeming Lamb, we enjoy Him day by day as the daily manna and the living rock. Later on there was the tabernacle with all its furniture. All these are types of the different aspects of Christ. Today we enjoy and experience Christ in the different aspects typified by the tabernacle and its different furniture.

This, however, is not all. After the children of Israel entered into Canaan, the manna stopped, and they had to eat the produce of the land (Josh. 5:12). When the children of Israel entered into Canaan, everything they needed for their living was taken from the land. They ate the things produced by this land, they drank something from this land, and they even had a building as their house from this land and on this land. Everything necessary for their living came out of this land. Hence, the good land is the all-inclusive type of Christ, that is, Christ as everything to us in an all-inclusive way.

TWO WAYS TO ENJOY
THE PRODUCE OF THE GOOD LAND

The enjoyment of the produce of the good land was definitely regulated and ordained by God. There were two ways for the children of Israel to enjoy the produce of the good land—the personal way and the corporate way.

We need to consider the passages from the book of Deuteronomy listed at the beginning of this chapter. On the one hand, the children of Israel had the full liberty to enjoy the produce in a personal way at any time and in any place. There was, however, another aspect, a corporate aspect. When they enjoyed the produce of the land of Canaan for their worship to God and for their fellowship with the people of God, they had to be regulated, ruled, and governed. They had no freedom to choose any place according to their desire. They had to go to the one place appointed, chosen, and ordained by God.

In these verses which we quoted from Deuteronomy, the phrase *the place which Jehovah will choose* occurs repeatedly. On the one hand, the children of Israel had the full liberty to enjoy the produce according to their desire, but that applied to only ninety percent of the produce. On the other hand, they had no right to enjoy the top one-tenth of their produce at any place of their choice. They had to bring all these things to the very place which the Lord chose or appointed. The appointed place of God's choice is a type, the significance of which we must see. If we are fair, we must apply all the types to Christ.

First, we know that the good land is a type of the all-inclusive Christ. Then the produce of Canaan is a type of the experiences of Christ. God gave the good land to the children of Israel, but they had to labor on it—they had to till the ground, sow the seed, reap the harvest, and take care of the herds and flocks. This typifies that since we have been transferred into Christ, who is the allotted portion of the saints in the light (Col. 1:12-13), we have to work, to labor, on Christ day by day. In the morning, we have to pray to Him and fellowship with Him. By laboring on Christ, we will have something produced out of Christ for our enjoyment. Many Christians, although they have Christ and are in Christ, are lazy. They do not labor on Christ. Day by day they neither pray nor have fellowship with Him. They do not have something out of Christ as their spiritual food to nourish their spiritual life. Due to their laziness, they have become poor.

Since we are in Christ and Christ is our portion, we have to cooperate with God by laboring on Christ, just as the children of Israel did. God gave the children of Israel the good land, and He also gave them the air, the rain, and the sunshine. They, however, had to cooperate with God by working on the land that they might have something produced from the land. All of the produce is a type of the experiences of Christ. If we labor on Christ and work together with Christ, we will have many things produced out of Christ as food to us for our enjoyment, and we will have a surplus of Christ.

As we mentioned earlier, there are two ways ordained by

God for His people to enjoy the produce of Christ. One way is that in our personal enjoyment of Christ we have the full liberty to enjoy anything of Christ at any time and in any place as our food for our own nourishment and spiritual supply. The second way to enjoy Christ is related to our corporate enjoyment. The children of Israel had no right, no freedom, to choose any place for them to bring their tithes, their burnt offerings, their heave offerings, and their vows to God as their worship to God in fellowship with God's people. They had to go to the place chosen by God.

MAINTAINING THE ONENESS OF GOD'S CHILDREN

Only in the place chosen, ordained, by God could the oneness of the children of Israel be kept and maintained. This means that when we enjoy Christ with God as our worship to God in the fellowship of His children, we have to be in the unique place ordained by God—the place of the oneness of God's children. Hence, it is clear that for us to enjoy Christ personally is one thing, and for us to enjoy Christ with others as a worship to God is another thing. For thousands of years in their history, the children of Israel had never been divided in their worship of God because they had no right to choose any place according to their desire. They had only one place where they could go to worship God in fellowship with one another. Even when the nation was divided into two, they were not allowed to have two places to worship God; they had only one place.

In the thousands of years of Israel's history throughout the generations, there have never been two temples built up for them to worship God. There has always been only one temple because there is only one place for the people to legitimately build the temple. One could not say, "You can build a temple in Jerusalem, so we can do the same thing in Babylon. Let us build the same thing with the same pattern, the same style, and the same materials, but in a different place." The temple in Jerusalem on the very piece of land appointed by God is right and acceptable to God. However, if one were to build exactly the same thing in another place, that would be wrong.

Suppose that after the children of Israel entered into the land of Canaan, there was not such a regulation about their worship to God. If they had had the freedom to choose any place for their worship to God, they would have been divided into many groups within a short time. The people of the tribe of Benjamin would have said, "We don't like to have the people from the tribe of Judah." Then the people of the tribe of Dan in the north would have said, "Since we are too far from Jerusalem and it is simply too inconvenient, let us build another place in our territory." Eventually, other tribes would follow and build other places within their own territories. This is the reason that, according to God's ordination, while they were free to enjoy the produce of the land for their personal enjoyment in any place, they were required to go to the unique place of God's choice to enjoy the top produce of the good land for the worship of God in fellowship with God's children. They had to keep the oneness of the people of God.

This signifies that for our personal enjoyment, we can enjoy Christ in any place at any time, but if we are going to enjoy Christ as our worship to God in fellowship with the other saints, we have to be careful because it affects our oneness. We do not have the freedom to do whatever is right in our eyes. If we disregard this, we will bring in divisions. There is only one place ordained, appointed, chosen, by God for His people to come together to share Christ with one another in the worship to the Father. This one place is the place of oneness. We have to keep the oneness in the worship to the Father in fellowship with one another. Otherwise, we will bring in divisions. I like the warning that is given in Deuteronomy 12:13: "Be careful that you do not offer up your burnt offerings in every place that you see." Brothers and sisters, be careful! This is a type which we must honor. We cannot apply other aspects concerning our experience of Christ and simply ignore this particular aspect. We have to apply this aspect too.

Suppose that I am a Hebrew in ancient times. For the whole year I labor diligently and have plenty of produce from the land for myself and my family to enjoy. For this we are really grateful to the Lord. Then I say to my wife and children,

"Dear wife and children, you know the Lord is so good to us. We have to worship Him. Let us go to Jerusalem and have a feast before Jehovah." My wife agrees with me wholeheartedly, but the children are against our going to Jerusalem because it is too far. Then I say, "All right, maybe it is better if we just go to our farm which is only one mile away from our house." So we go to our farm and even invite some of our neighbors to join us. We say to ourselves, "How nice it is that we do not have to travel such a long distance to Jerusalem. We can just worship God right where we are since God is everywhere. Let us enjoy the tithes. Let us also set up an altar and put all the burnt offerings and the heave offerings on the altar. If they can build an altar in Jerusalem, why can we not do the same here in our place? This is very nice and very convenient."

Then another Hebrew will hear about what we are doing, and he will decide to gather some of his neighbors to do the same thing. Eventually, the people of Israel will be automatically and spontaneously divided, and there will be no end to their divisions. However, God did not allow this for the children of Israel. They were regulated strictly by God in their worship to Him; three times a year they had to go to worship God in the place which God chose (Deut. 16:16). If they offered their offerings in other places, that would be considered sinful to God.

We need to apply this type to ourselves. The place of oneness is the unique ground or standing of oneness. When you go to any city, you do not have the freedom to set up any meeting you like for the worship or service of God. You have to be limited, ruled, and regulated. This is the church life. This is the reason why many people do not feel happy to talk about the church life, because with the church life there is limitation.

When we talk about our personal enjoyment of Christ, everything is so nice because we are absolutely free to enjoy Him wherever we are. The Lord is the Spirit, who is everywhere, so we can enjoy Him without any limitation. But do you think that as Christians we have the liberty to do whatever we like in our worship to God in the enjoyment of

Christ in fellowship with others? This is the misuse of freedom in the church's history. It seems today that it is easy for any Christian to set up a meeting. If you can come to Los Angeles to set up a meeting, so can I. You and I, however, need to consider that if we do this, we just bring in more divisions and thereby damage the oneness of God's children.

Suppose a brother who is of the tribe of Benjamin has been offended by a brother who is of the tribe of Judah. When the Feast of Tabernacles comes, the brother from the tribe of Benjamin does not feel happy about going to Jerusalem since the brother who has offended him is also going there. What can the Benjaminite do? Can he set up an altar on his farm and offer his tithes and burnt offerings there? The answer, of course, is no. Here is a picture of the test to the flesh and to the natural intention. Here is the need of the application of the cross to the natural man.

But look at the situation today. When people cannot get along with others or do not feel happy about one another, they just set up different meetings according to their taste or preference. Where is the limitation to the flesh? Where is the regulation to the natural man? There is nothing limiting or regulating people. Every man does whatever is right in his eyes. Everyone can offer his burnt offerings in any place he chooses. So the oneness of the people of God is gone. As a result, there are all kinds of complications and divisions. We need to have a real repentance before God.

Do we really know the right ground for the children of God to worship God with Christ in the fellowship with one another? We should not be more liberal than what has been ordained by God. We have to keep the oneness. This is why many times, by the mercy of the Lord, I have declared to the Lord's children that they have no right to form anything, to start anything, according to their own convenience and preference. There is only one proper ground for the Lord's children to share Christ with one another in fellowship as a worship to the Father. That proper ground is the ground of oneness.

Suppose you come to Los Angeles, and there is already a group of believers meeting together on the proper ground in worshipping God and in fellowshipping with one another.

Then you do not have the freedom to set up another meeting. You have to submit to them because there is only one ground of oneness, one place ordained, appointed, by God for His people to worship Him and share His Christ in fellowship with one another. If you start another meeting according to what you prefer, you simply break the regulation, the rule, of the oneness of the Lord's people.

In the history of the Jewish nation, there was a person who did this thing. His name was Jeroboam. Jeroboam not only divided the nation but also tried his best to divide the people's worship to God (1 Kings 12:20-33). By this he damaged the oneness of God's people and brought in a great curse from God (14:6-16).

For the practice of the church life, we need to learn to take care of the oneness. If we give up the ground of the oneness of the Body of Christ, there is no need for us to talk about the church life. If we do whatever is right in our eyes, any talk about the church life is meaningless. If we mean business to practice the church life, we have to make a definite decision concerning the proper ground of oneness.

COMING WITH SOMETHING OF CHRIST
FOR OUR FELLOWSHIP WITH ONE ANOTHER

Now we need to go further and consider another thing. Whenever we come together to worship God in sharing Christ in fellowship with one another, we have to come with something of Christ. We should not come with our hands empty. There were only two rules for the people of Israel in their coming together to worship God. One was that they had no right to choose the place of worship, but they had to take the place chosen by God. The other was that they were not allowed to come with their hands empty, but they had to come with their hands filled with the produce of the good land (Deut. 16:16-17). Today this means that whenever we come to the meeting with others to worship God by sharing Christ in fellowship with one another, we have to bring something of Christ as a surplus in our hands.

In ancient times when the children of Israel came together three times a year, at the Feast of Unleavened Bread, the

Feast of Weeks, and the Feast of Tabernacles, that was a big exhibition of all the different kinds of rich produce of the good land. This is a type. Whenever we come together, we have to come with our hands filled with Christ. When we all come in this way, we have an exhibition of Christ. We have the proper ground of oneness for the worship of God, and we also have the reality of the riches of Christ for the worship of God. All the surplus of the produce of the good land of Canaan was not only for the enjoyment of the children of Israel but also for the enjoyment of God. God enjoyed all the things together with His people. Likewise, we have to bring Christ into our worship of God and let God enjoy Christ with us. When we share Christ with one another, we offer Christ to God as an enjoyment to Him.

The situation today, however, is pitiful. On the one hand, there are divisions upon divisions, and on the other hand, there are empty hands upon empty hands. We need to come back to the proper situation revealed in the Scriptures. On the one hand, we have to keep the oneness of the Lord's people, and on the other hand, we have to be full of the surplus of Christ in our hands. Whenever we come together, we come with an abundance of Christ. In our gatherings a sister could give a testimony telling us how Christ is her strength in her sufferings, and a brother could testify of how he has experienced Christ as his joy. Then others, one by one, could testify something about their experience of Christ. This is a meeting full of the exhibition of Christ. This is also the real practice of the church life acceptable and well pleasing to God the Father.

DAILY LABORING ON CHRIST

But how can we be full of Christ? This depends on our daily laboring on Christ. We have to labor, to work, on Christ. Without laboring on Christ, we will have nothing to share with one another when we come together. Since we have nothing of Christ, our worship will be a poor worship. However, if we labor on Christ, if we experience Him day by day, fellowship with Him, and pray to Him, we will come together with the surplus of Christ. When we come to the meeting, we will have something to offer, to contribute. We will be able to say, "Father, here is something of Your Son whom I have experienced; I offer Him to You." We will also be able to share what we have experienced of Christ with others, and others will also do the same. This is the real worship.

The real worship today is that when we come together, we come with something of Christ to offer to the Father and to share with others. This is the real worship that is well pleasing to the Father. Even while we are preaching Christ and ministering Christ to the sinners, this kind of preaching, this kind of ministry, is the real worship to the Father. Whenever we share Christ with others, we render the real worship to the Father. Without offering Christ to the Father and without sharing Christ with others, our worship to God cannot be well pleasing to Him. When we enjoy Christ with the Father and let the Father enjoy Christ with us, this is the genuine worship.

Do you know the difference between the worship of God rendered by the angels and that rendered by Christians? The angels prostrate themselves or bow down before God to worship God, but there is no need for us Christians to do that. In our spirit we realize that the proper worship for us Christians today is to bring Christ to offer to God the Father. We let the Father enjoy His Son with us, and we also enjoy Christ with one another in fellowship.

This depends on our daily experience of Christ. We have to labor on Christ day and night and let Christ give us a lot of produce. Then we will have rich experiences of Christ which not only are enough to take care of our need, but also allow us to have a tithe, a surplus, to bring to God and to serve others. Whenever we meet on the proper ground of oneness in this way, we have an exhibition of Christ. This is the glory and worship to the Father, the enjoyment to the saints, and the shame to the enemy. This is the church life.

Let us learn something from the type of the good land. We are in Christ. We have to experience Him diligently that we may have plenty of Christ for our personal enjoyment and also have a surplus for us to offer to God and share with others. Then we have to come together by taking care of the oneness of the Lord's children. The proper and real church life is the life of a corporate body meeting together on the proper ground of oneness with the fullness of Christ for the worship of God and fellowship with others.

CHAPTER FIFTEEN

ONENESS AND CHRIST

(1)

Scripture Reading: Deut. 12:5, 8, 11, 13, 27; 14:22-23

I would like to stress again the type of the living of God's people in the good land. The types in the Old Testament are the figures, the pictures, of the spiritual things. In the New Testament we have the teachings and the words about the spiritual things. We all know that a picture is always clearer than any kind of statement. This is why there is a saying that a picture is better than a thousand words. The whole Scripture is one. The Old Testament and the New Testament reveal to us the same thing. Whereas the Old Testament gives us the pictures, the New Testament gives us the statements. When we are not so clear about the statements, we have to look at the pictures.

KEEPING THE ONENESS

The two main things concerning the living of God's people in the good land can be simply stated with two words: oneness and Christ. The life of the children of Israel in the good land as God's people is a life of worship to God. In this life of worship to God, two things are necessary. The first thing is to keep the oneness of the Lord's people. You should not do anything to damage the oneness. Once the oneness is damaged, the proper worship to God is also gone. If any division exists, there is no possibility to have a proper worship that is acceptable and well pleasing to God. This is a serious matter today.

In the Old Testament we see that throughout the generations the worship rendered by the children of Israel to God was never divided. They never had two temples built up in two places at the same time. There has always been one temple, one center for worship. This is not just a matter of geography. This is a matter of oneness. The oneness of the people of God was always preserved, kept, maintained, in the worship of God. This is because whenever the oneness of the Lord's children is damaged and spoiled, the building is impossible. The building of the church, the temple of God, the Body of Christ, depends upon oneness.

Furthermore, today under the light of the Holy Spirit in the New Testament, we know that the oneness is the biggest test to our flesh, our natural man, and our soulish life. To find out whether or not you are fleshly, natural, soulish, or worldly, you need to ask yourself just one question: "Am I willing to keep the oneness of the Body?"

Suppose six young brothers in a certain city come and meet together. In the beginning it is wonderful, but perhaps after three weeks, one of them may feel unhappy about the others. Then he may seek out another three or five to pray with him, and eventually they may decide to meet as another meeting. So probably within half a year, in your city there will be two separate meetings. This means division. Deuteronomy 12:8 says, "...each man doing all that is right in his own eyes." But the oneness limits this. The oneness will not allow you to do whatever is right in your own eyes. Regardless of whether you feel happy about others or whether they are spiritual or not, you have to keep the oneness with them. You have no right to separate yourself from others. This regulation preserves the oneness of the children of God.

As students, you have a choice of schools. If you are not happy about one school, you can quit and go to another school. But as a Christian, do you have a choice of churches? Today many Christians are frequently changing churches. When one church does not suit their taste, they leave that one and go to another one. When the second church does not suit their taste, they leave again and go to a third one. We must realize that as far as the church is concerned, we must give up our taste. We cannot have a church according to our taste. We have no choice as far as the church is concerned. We have to take what God has appointed, ordained, chosen, to keep the oneness of the Body. This is the biggest test to our flesh, our natural man.

Do you believe that all the members of the church are wonderful persons? It seems that the members of the Body, the saved ones, are peculiar people. This means that according to the flesh, according to the natural man, it is not easy to be together with the believers. Unless you learn the lessons, sooner or later, you will drop out. With the matter of the church there is no choice. This requires us to learn how to fear the Lord and deal with our flesh.

In 1926 Brother Watchman Nee started to work in Shanghai to establish the church there. Later, in 1942 the enemy raised up a big turmoil in the church in Shanghai. Brother Nee was put in a position that he could no longer minister there. Some of the saints came to Brother Nee, saying, "Brother Nee, let us have another start. Let us start another meeting." Brother Nee told them, "No. You have to continue going to that meeting. No matter what kind of attitude they have toward you or toward me, you have to go to that meeting. That is the church. Neither you nor I have the right to start another thing." This is the test to the self, to the soul-life. This is the biggest lesson.

Today it is very easy for the believers to form meetings. Many believers who are dissatisfied with the so-called traditional church service just meet in their homes. They think everyone has the right to set up a meeting. They are too free. There is no limitation, no rule. I once went to a certain city and met with at least three or four free groups. They all claimed that they were non-sectarian, yet they would not come together to be one with one another. Every group keeps itself independent, separate, from the others. Strictly speaking, this is lawlessness. There is no regulation, no rule. We should not be legalistic, but we should not be too liberal either. We need to be governed, ruled.

The proper governing rule or principle is the oneness. Suppose there are some brothers in a certain locality. They start to meet in the name of the Lord on the proper ground of oneness. When I go to their city, I have no right to set up another meeting. I have to keep the oneness with them. Right away, however, I am put on the test because human beings always like to take the lead. If I had started the meeting there, I might have been number one. But now that I come here to meet with them, I would be number two. Everyone likes to be the king. Because I do not want to be the second but the first, I would not submit to their meeting. Rather, I would set up another meeting so that I may be a little king. If there is not the grace and the lesson of the cross, everyone of us would be like this. But here is the test. If we are going to keep the oneness of the Body, we do not have a choice. There are many lessons for us to learn in order to keep the oneness.

Look at today's situation among the Christians. There are divisions after divisions because of the flesh, the self, and the natural man. There are the state churches and the denominational churches. Following this, there is the Brethren practice. Then today there are so many free groups. Today the practice of the free groups is fashionable. They say that they are really free from the denominational system, but the divisions created by the free groups are endless. If I do not agree with you who are meeting on Twenty-third Street, I will set up a meeting on Twenty-fifth Street. If I am not satisfied with the meeting that is in your home, I will set up a meeting in my home. This is too free. The free groups simply neglect the oneness of the Body of Christ. We have to honor this ground of oneness.

Do you think there is a proper reason for you to separate yourself from other Christians meeting in the Lord's name on the ground of oneness? No reason is proper, and no reason is valid. As long as you live in Israel, you have to go together with all of Israel to worship God. You have no choice but to do it. If you would not do it, that means you break the law and you have become lawless. Suppose you and another Israelite are enemies. It is a real problem. You and he, according to the law, have to go to the same place three times a year to worship God. This is a real test. Therefore, you have to forgive him, and he has to forgive you. You have to learn how to be happy with him by the Lord's grace, and he has to learn to be happy with you. You have to keep the oneness. I believe this is clear to all of us.

EXPERIENCING CHRIST

Now we come to the second main thing in the living of God's people in the good land, and that is Christ. When you come as an Israelite to worship God, you have to bring the produce of the land of Canaan. We know that the different sorts of produce are types of the different aspects of Christ. You have to bring Christ to the worship of God. This is also a governing principle.

Whenever we come together, we have to bring Christ. Do not bring anything else. What you need to bring to the meeting must be Christ or some aspects of Christ. Do not bring your doctrines, your opinions, or your interpretations. Rather, bring something of Christ. Suppose a brother brings the debate about predestination to the meeting. Is that something of Christ? You and I have to learn the lesson strictly. Whenever we come to the meeting, what we bring must be Christ Himself. Look at the picture in ancient times. When the people of Israel came together to worship God, they just brought the produce of the good land of Canaan to offer to God. What they offered to God would be the food to God for His satisfaction and enjoyment. Also, they shared with one another all that they had offered to God. We are clear today that all the offerings, all the things offered to God, are types of Christ.

Concerning the offerings, let me give you a summary. All the offerings are classified into two main categories. One is the offerings of the animal life, and the other is the offerings of the vegetable life. The Israelites offered something of the herd and of the flocks, which are things of the animal life. They also offered corn, wheat, wine, and oil, which are things of the vegetable life.

There are also two aspects of the life of Christ. The first aspect is that His life is likened to the animal life, which typifies the redeeming life. Whenever you offer something of the herd or of the flock, that will be slain and the blood will be shed. With the shedding of the blood, there is the redeeming (Heb. 9:22, 12). With Christ the Lord, His life in the first aspect is a redeeming life, which is typified by the animal life. The other aspect of the Lord's life is the generating life, which is typified by the vegetable life. A grain of wheat falls into the earth and dies, and when it grows up it produces many grains (John 12:24). This means it generates. This is why I say the vegetable life is a generating life.

The life of Christ, on the one hand, is the redeeming life to redeem us, and on the other hand, is the generating life to generate much fruit. Our experiences of Christ can be classified into these two categories. Christ as the redeeming life recovers, heals, cures, and restores us. Then there are many other times when we experience Christ as the generating life that generates us, resurrects us, gives life to us, energizes us, strengthens us, and empowers us. The life of Christ is a powerful life that strengthens and energizes us that through us something may be produced. Therefore, in our experience of Christ we should have many flocks and herds and also much wine, oil, corn, and wheat.

All the saints bring all these experiences of Christ to the meeting and offer them to God. In a certain sense, these experiences may be considered as a burnt offering. The burnt offering is something offered to God for God's satisfaction. There were five main offerings in the Old Testament—the burnt offering, the meal offering, the peace offering, the sin offering, and the trespass offering. Christ as the burnt offering is for the satisfaction of God.

Also, what we bring to God may be considered as a heave offering. To heave means to lift up. Therefore, the heave offering typifies the ascended Christ. Christ, who has accomplished everything, is the ascended One, the lifted-up One. On the one hand, as the burnt offering, Christ is the very satisfaction to God. On the other hand, as the heave offering, Christ is the ascended One who has accomplished everything. Whenever we come to the meeting, we have to bring these kinds of experiences of Christ.

When the early Christians came together, do you believe they came with predestination, with Calvinism, or with Arminianism? Of course not. Rather, they came with the

Christ whom they experienced and offered to God as the burnt offering for God's satisfaction and as the heave offering, as the One who has accomplished everything and ascended to the heavens. Today let us learn how to experience Christ in such a way.

In order to practice the church life, we do not need to learn some technical matters. We must know that the way to practice the church life is to experience Christ daily. Everyone of us has to experience Christ daily so that whenever we come to the meeting we come with something of Christ. Then we will have much of Christ to offer to God as the heave offering, as the One who has accomplished everything, and also as the burnt offering, as the satisfaction to God.

The building of the temple and the city can come about only by these offerings. If you keep coming together with your hands empty, with nothing to bring to God as the offerings, nothing will be built up. The building depends on the offering, and the offering depends on the daily laboring on the good land. The building of the church depends on our offering of Christ, and our offering of Christ in the meetings depends on our experiences of Christ in our daily life. We need to experience Christ by laboring on Him; then we will have something to bring to the meetings to contribute to others and to share with God. By this kind of offering the building will be accomplished.

We come together to meet, time after time, with the expectation that the church might be built up. But if we are going to be built up, we need some material. We may say that we believers are the material, but actually in ourselves we are the garbage. We need to be hauled away by the garbage truck. Do not think that we could be used as material for the building up of the Body of Christ. We need to be buried. The material for the building is the Christ whom we have experienced. If we keep coming to meet again and again without something of Christ to contribute to others, there cannot be any building. If we come to the meeting with nothing of Christ but with a lot of rubbish—the natural life, the self, the flesh, and the worldly things—how can we be built up?

The building of the city and the temple came out of the offerings. The more the people offered, the more material they had to build up the city and the temple. Their offerings depended on their daily laboring on the good land. Today it is the same. We have Christ, and we are in Christ. Christ is a very rich, good land, but we are lazy. We would not pay the price to cooperate with Christ. We would not labor on Christ. So when we come to the meetings, we come empty-handed. Meeting after meeting we are empty and have nothing to be built up with. Do not think that just by coming together we can be built up. To be built up there is the need of some material.

This is why in the New Testament the apostles Paul, Peter, and even John all conveyed the same message that we have to grow up into Christ that we may have some measure of Christ's stature for the building up of the Body. Ephesians 4 shows that growth and maturity are needed so that we can have some stature of Christ (vv. 13, 15-16). It is only by the increase of Christ within us for our growth in Christ that the Body of Christ can be built up. We have to be transformed by Christ that we may have the stature of Christ. We cannot build up the church by meeting with empty hands. We must work on Christ to have the experiences of Christ.

Let us look at the picture in the Old Testament. Suppose all the children of Israel were lazy. They had a piece of the good land, yet they did not work on the land. No one would till the ground, sow the seed, or take care of the harvest. Everyone just had a good time. They had no herds, no flocks, no wine, no oil, no corn, and no wheat. Then when it was time to go to the feasts, everyone would go empty-handed. They had no food for God nor for themselves. God was hungry, and they were also hungry. Eventually, there would be no material for the building up of the city and the temple.

This is the real situation of the poor church today. Many times this is the condition of our poor meetings. We come to the meeting with nothing of Christ, and we expect others to have something of Christ to share. The brothers come with the hope that the sisters will have something to share, and the sisters come with the expectation that the brothers will have something to share. Eventually, nobody has anything to share, and the meeting becomes an empty meeting because we do not labor on Christ.

What is the way to practice the church? First, we have to realize that there is the need of oneness, and second, we have to realize that there is the need to have many experiences of Christ. We have to experience Christ all the time. Then we will have something in our hands of Christ as food for ourselves and for the needy ones. We will also have something of Christ to offer to God to satisfy God as a burnt offering and as a heave offering. Then there will be the material to build up a dwelling place for God. The proper way for us to practice the church life is to respect the oneness and to experience Christ in order to have a surplus of Christ to bring to the church to share with the saints in the worship of God so that God can be satisfied with Christ and enjoy Christ with us. Then we will have something built up. Besides this, there is no other way to practice the proper church life and to build up the church as the living expression of Christ.

There is the urgent need for us to experience Christ, to minister Christ to others, and to help others to know Christ. Without Christ there is no gold, silver, pearl, or precious stones. Without Christ there is no material for the building up of the Body. Without Christ you have wood, grass, and stubble, which are not good for the building up of the Body (1 Cor. 3:12).

There is a great need of prayer for this matter. I hope that we will pray for this matter of experiencing Christ for the building up of the Body. We cannot just learn the technique of practicing the church. If all we have is technique, we just have an empty church, a church without reality. The reality of the church is the very Christ experienced by us. This very Christ is the contents of the real worship to God and the material for the building up of the church. I would urge all of us to pray much about this matter.

3-26-95C

Chapter Sixteen

ONENESS AND CHRIST

(2)

Scripture Reading: Psa. 133

THE WAY TO PRACTICE THE CHURCH LIFE AS SEEN IN PSALM 133

In this chapter we want to continue our fellowship concerning the need to keep the oneness and experience Christ for the practice of the church life. Let us read Psalm 133: "Behold, how good and how pleasant it is / For brothers to dwell in oneness! / It is like the fine oil upon the head / That ran down upon the beard, / Upon Aaron's beard, / That ran down to the hem of his garments; / Like the dew of Hermon / That came down upon the mountains of Zion. / For there Jehovah commanded the blessing: / Life forever" (Heb.).

In this short psalm of three verses, there are four important things expressed by four words: first, oneness; second, oil; third, dew; and fourth, life. The way to practice the church is in these four things: the oneness, the oil, the dew, and the life.

This psalm is one of fifteen psalms, from Psalm 120 to 134, which are called Songs of Ascent. These are songs chanted by the children of Israel while they were coming together and going up to Mount Zion to worship God. They did this three times a year at the Feast of Unleavened Bread, the Feast of Weeks, and the Feast of Tabernacles (Deut. 16:16). Hence, these songs were the songs for their meetings. Even though the church was not in the Old Testament, the people of Israel were a type of the church. In particular, Psalm 133 is related to the way of the practice of the church life.

In the previous chapter, we saw two things that are crucial

to the practice of the church life. One thing is the oneness as the ground of the church life, and the other is Christ as the reality of the church life. We need the ground and the reality as well. If we invite people for dinner, we need a table and also a lot of food. We cannot just serve people a table without the food, nor can we serve people the food without a table. The proper church life is a life of a proper ground, which is the oneness, and of the reality, which is Christ.

Some have advised me not to talk too much about the ground of the church and to just talk about Christ, the reality. They appreciated the Lord's presence and the reality, but they did not want to speak about the ground of the church. I said to them, "What you appreciate may be likened to tea. You drink the tea, yet you don't appreciate the teacup. It seems that you are saying, 'Tea is so nice, but the cup is not good for drinking.' Yes, I know the cup is not good for drinking, but you need a cup to put the tea in. To serve tea, you need the cup as well as the tea. Likewise, to practice the church, we need the ground as well as the reality of the church."

THE ONENESS

I appreciate Psalm 133. Verse 1 says, "Behold, how good and how pleasant it is / For brothers to dwell in oneness!" They kept the oneness by coming to the one place appointed, chosen, ordained, by God. No one had the right to set up another place for their coming together to worship God. Their worship to God was kept as one for generations and generations because they kept the ground of oneness.

THE ANOINTING OIL

We also need the reality, which according to Psalm 133 includes the oil, the dew, and the life. Do we have the oil in our meetings? The anointing oil is nothing less than the all-inclusive Spirit of Christ. Whenever we come together, we must have the all-inclusive Christ as the Spirit moving and working through us and among us. In the meetings of the churches, there must be the flow of the Spirit. There must be the anointing, which is the working, the moving, the flowing, of the Spirit among the saints. This needs our daily practice of experiencing Christ.

Psalm 133 tells us that the anointing oil was on the head of Aaron, the high priest, and that it ran down upon his beard to the hem of his garments. That means the anointing oil flows down to the whole body. This is the stream, the current, the flow, of the Spirit. This signifies simply that whenever we have the expression of the Body of Christ, there must be a flow of the Holy Spirit upon all the members, upon the whole Body.

Many times at the Lord's table, I had the sense that the flow of the Spirit started from a certain brother and flowed through another brother, but was not able to pass through a third brother. This is because the third one was not in the spirit. The meetings will expose where you are as a Christian. Suppose a brother is worldly, carnal, and not loving the Lord, yet he comes to the meeting. There is something within him as a hindrance to the flow of the Spirit. This proves that this member is not much in the spirit. If all the attendants of the meeting are in such a condition, the Spirit cannot get through, and there is no flow, no anointing, in the meeting. Then the meeting becomes very dry.

When we live in Christ throughout our daily living, we come to the meetings with part of Christ, and that part of Christ is a part of the anointing oil. I come with a part of Christ, with some experience of Christ, and this experience of Christ is a part of the anointing oil. If we all come in this way, we will have the flow of the Spirit. This flow proves that we are in the proper practice of the church life. Sometimes a number of brothers and sisters will be convicted by this flow. This flow of the Spirit is the reality of the practice of the church life.

THE DEW AS THE REFRESHING GRACE

The dew in Psalm 133 is a type of grace. In Proverbs we are told that the king's favor, or grace, is as dew upon the grass (19:12b). Where you have the morning dew, you have the refreshing and the newness. This is the refreshing grace of God, which in our experience is the presence of God.

Whenever the saints come to meet together to practice the church life, there should be the freshness, the newness, and the refreshing of the Lord's presence. Most of our meetings are held in the evening, yet when we are in the meetings, we feel as if it were morning. We have the newness and sense that the Lord's presence is so refreshing. That is the dew—the refreshing of the grace of the Lord's presence.

When we come together, a young sister who was baptized only two weeks ago may give a short prayer. That short prayer is at least a drop of dew that refreshes and brings in the newness. Many times before I went to the meeting, I was really tired. But after a short prayer by a sister, I immediately was refreshed. That is the presence of the Lord as the dew of grace to us.

Sometimes, however, when we come to a meeting, we sense the dryness. There is no anointing, no oil, and no refreshing, no dew. The anointing and the refreshing are the Lord Himself. Therefore, the content of our meeting life depends on the saints' experience of Christ in their daily life. It does not depend merely on a few responsible brothers, but on the whole congregation, on every brother and sister. By this anointing and this dew we have the blessing commanded by the Lord (Psa. 133:3b). This blessing is life—life forever, life eternal.

Brothers and sisters, I would beg you to try your best to forget about the doctrines. The Christian meetings are not for doctrines but for the vision of Christ. Some have asked me, "Brother Lee, if you do not have the doctrines, how could you have the meetings?" This depends on what kind of doctrines you have. If you have some doctrines or teachings ministering Christ, this is right. However, we should never have a meeting for any kind of doctrine other than Christ Himself. If you come to the meeting and bring the doctrine of predestination without ministering Christ to others, this is wrong. We should always keep in mind that the church meetings are not for anything else but for the exhibition of Christ. If you have something of the Spirit and of Christ to minister to others, that is right and you have to do it. But never bring something simply as a doctrine to discuss, argue, or debate about. This will bring death to the meeting. You will not have the anointing, the dew, and the life. I hope that all the meetings of the local churches will be meetings full of Christ, full of the Spirit, full of the flow of the anointing, full of the dew, and full of life.

I say again that all this depends on our daily life, our daily experience of Christ and of the Spirit. When we come to the meetings, we must have our hands full of Christ to share with others, to contribute to others, and to minister to others, while at the same time, we hope to receive some help from others as our food supply in the Spirit.

TWO THINGS THAT SPOIL THE CHURCH LIFE

There are two things that spoil the church life. One is the fact that there are so many different grounds. Today people are liberal to have many different meetings. This kind of liberal attitude spoils and damages the church life. How could you say, "Behold, how good and how pleasant it is for brothers to dwell in oneness"? You cannot say this because the oneness is gone. We are in the same city, and even in the same part of the city, yet we have three or four different groups. There are too many grounds. The unique ground is spoiled, so it is hard to have the real church life.

Then the other thing that spoils the church life is that whenever the saints come together, they always desire to know and pay attention to something other than Christ. Therefore, there is no ground of oneness and no reality of Christ. Consequently, the church life is gone.

If we are going to practice the church life in a proper way, first, we have to clear the ground. Our flesh, our desire, and our taste have to be dealt with by the cross. We have to respect the ground of oneness. In other words, we have to respect the oneness of the Body. We have no right to choose a ground to set up a meeting. We can only take the ground appointed by God.

Furthermore, we cannot have an empty cup, that is, an empty ground. We must be filled with Christ and the Spirit. This depends on our daily experience. We should not expect that whenever we meet together, the Spirit will come down from the heavens and be poured upon us. This is a dream. We must be awakened out of our dreaming. The right way is that each of us has to deal with the Lord, to have fellowship with Him, to be dealt with by Him, to be filled by Him, and to be occupied by Him in our daily life. We experience Christ, we learn the lesson of the cross, and we walk in the spirit with Christ. Then when we come to the meeting, we come with something of Christ. Spontaneously, we have something to share with the saints, something to offer to God to satisfy Him, and something to minister to others.

This is to function in the meetings by ministering Christ to others. You may not be able to give a message, but you can give a short prayer or a short testimony. If you are in the spirit and you have some experience of Christ, whenever you open your mouth, Christ will be offered and manifested by and in your prayer. We all have to experience Christ in this way. Then whenever we come together, something of Christ will be brought together and will be manifested. Eventually, the building up of the Body will be realized, because only the Christ experienced by us is the real material for the building of the church.

We may attend meetings throughout the year, but unless we have the adequate experience of Christ, we still will not be able to have any kind of building. When we experience Christ in a rich way, we have much of Christ to bring to the meetings, to share with one another, to exhibit, to glorify God, and to put the enemy to shame. Then this Christ whom we experienced will be the material for the building up of the church. We believers can never be built up together in ourselves. We can be built up together only in Christ, with Christ, and by Christ.

We mentioned before that the city and the temple in Jerusalem came into existence through the offerings brought by the children of Israel. If they had had nothing to offer, there would have been no material for the building of the city and the temple. The offerings were the produce of the good land. They were the fruit of the labor of the children of Israel. This is a type.

If we are going to have a church built up practically in

our area, there is the need for a group of believers who live by taking Christ as everything. They walk in the spirit and practice this kind of life day by day. Hence, they are filled with Christ and have much of Christ in their hands. Whenever they come together, everyone has something of Christ to contribute to the meeting and offer to God. Furthermore, they keep this one regulation, that is, they keep the oneness and stay away from any kind of division. They concentrate all their experiences of Christ together as material for the building of the church. Eventually, something of Christ will be built up together as a real building to be a practical, living expression of Christ. This is the way to practice the church life.

Let us pray much about this matter so that we may realize the life and the way for the practice of the church life. Let us pray that a real building of the church may be realized in our area and even in the entire United States.